Adult
Children
of
Divorce

Adult Children of Divorce

Haunting Problems and Healthy Solutions

KAREN J. SANDVIG

WORD PUBLISHING
Dallas·London·Vancouver·Melbourne

ADULT CHILDREN OF DIVORCE

Copyright © 1990 by Karen Sandvig

Library of Congress Cataloging in Publication Data

Sandvig, Karen J. 1956–
    Adult children of divorce : haunting problems and healthy solutions /
by Karen J. Sandvig.
      p.   cm.
    Includes bibliographical references.
    ISBN 0-8499-3222-X
    1. Adult children of divorced parents—Mental health. I. Title.
RC569.5.A3S36 1990
155.9'24—dc20   90-12714
                                                CIP

Printed in the United States of America
012349MP10987654321

This one is for the children.
Please, God, hold them in Your arms
and love them to wholeness.

Mark 10:14
"Jesus . . . said to them,
'Let the little children come to me,
and do not hinder them,
for the kingdom of God belongs to such as these.'"

Contents

Introduction

I remember trying to climb to the top of a huge sand pile when I was a small child. At first I tried simply to walk up it like a staircase. But with each footstep the sand shifted and I just couldn't make much progress upward. Getting frustrated, I moved several feet away from the sand pile and blasted toward it with all my might. No real success. I tried again. And again.

I'd make it as much as half-way up and then the sands would grasp my feet and stop me short. I stood at the half-way point and the sand carried me backward — toward the ground.

However, I was a persistent child and I was not going to be defeated by this sand pile. I took off my shoes, pushed out my chin, and crept slowly toward the large mound as if to take it by surprise. I curled my bare toes into the sand, clawed with my fingernails, and slowly crawled upward. The sands still shifted sometimes and I lost ground, but inch-by-inch I got to the top of the stubborn old sand pile. I sat there, my face toward the warm sun, and grinned from ear to ear!

Life is often like climbing a huge sand pile for a particularly vast segment of contemporary society—the adult children of divorce (ACDs). Kids from the first generational wave of divorced families have grown up. And many have problems to deal with in adulthood that are strongly rooted in the emotional tangles of their parents' divorces.

Half of all marriages end in divorce.[1] Many couples who divorce are parents. There are millions of little children from broken families who grow up to be adult children with long-term effects on their personalities and lives.

If parents split a marriage in two—no matter how imperfect that marriage might have been—the sands of life shift dramatically for children. They are often tumbled down toward the hard ground, feeling abandoned, confused, fearful, and depressed.

Kids usually survive the fall and instinctively strive to reach the warmth and security of the top of the sand pile of life. Unfortunately, however, many ACDs try over and over to climb the sand pile without success.

Only when you dig into life with your bare hands and feet—facing honestly the effects of your parents' divorce and coping with leftover problems and scars—can you inch your way toward the top of the pile. It can be a painful struggle for many months or years, but it is necessary and worth it to feel the sun on your face and a grin in your heart!

Climbing the sand pile can be especially difficult because you may be carrying heavy emotional burdens—twenty-four hours a day, seven days a week—from your childhood, particularly from the time just preceding, during, and after your parents' divorce. I call this weight the "Piggy-Back Child."

The Piggy-Back Child is a part of you, emotional baggage you don't need to carry around because it weighs you down and inhibits the joy in your life.

Carrying the Piggy-Back Child is very difficult to do in the best of circumstances, but even more so when trying to crawl up the shifting sand piles of life.

Wherever you go, the Piggy-Back Child goes along. Depending on what kinds of issues you carry into adulthood that affect your personality, the Piggy-Back Child may feel as heavy as a toddler, an elementary-aged child, or a big adolescent.

You may become so used to carrying your extra burden that you don't consciously notice it. But sometimes an issue arises or a crisis happens and the Piggy-Back Child gets a stranglehold on you, letting all his weight hang from your neck.

You may have worked on your personal problems, you may even have gone for professional counseling, and you think the Piggy-Back Child has dismounted for good. Then, something comes up and you discover that he's there — pulling around your ankles or tugging on your arms, begging to climb aboard for another ride.

The nice thing about the Piggy-Back Child is that he is not permanent. No matter how many times you become aware that he's on your back or how badly he wants to stay there, you can coax him off successfully. He's simply a pesky hitchhiker. You control how long he stays with you, where you take him, how much he affects you, what power you allow him to have in your life, and when you choose to integrate him into your whole personality.

Because the Piggy-Back Child is a part of you, he is there at certain moments, during certain time frames, and in certain circumstances throughout your life. He may get frightened when someone yells at you and hug his legs around your stomach. When somebody tries to force you to do something against your will he may get angry and scratch on your shoulders.

Some people try to deny that they have any personal hang-ups. They may try to pretend that they don't have a Piggy-Back Child. But that's usually wrong. Most of us have a Piggy-Back Child that rides into adulthood with us in some way or another. It may be a problem with anger, jealousy, insecurity, or self-esteem; but the Piggy-Back Child usually makes his presence known in a variety of symptoms and relationships.

In this book we'll look at the different ways that the Piggy-Back Child exercises power in our lives and how we allow him to cause us misery. Real people who are struggling to overcome the ten most prevalent problems for adult children of divorce share how they are managing and coping with them.

From more than 300 surveys and 125 personal contacts with ACDs in nearly every walk of life, region of the country, and ranging in age from their early twenties to their sixties, I have gleaned a tremendous amount of valuable information about what it's like to be an adult who has grown up in the aftermath of a divorce.

This book is not a judgment against divorce. It is not written to give ACDs an easy way to dump personal adult problems onto the sometimes still smoldering ashes of parents' divorces. Rather, it shares vital information, gives many examples, tips, practical suggestions, and advice that will help you understand the special kinds of pain, vulnerability, and pressures with which adult children of divorce must often live.

I would like to thank the many people who have been brave enough and kind enough to share their special hurts and fears with me so that others may better understand themselves or those close to them.

By becoming aware of why ACDs believe, act, or feel the way they do about different areas of their lives after growing up with parents who were divorced, you can reach a higher ground of wisdom and understanding about the choices your parents, siblings, and other loved ones made that ultimately affected the person you are today. Armed with new awareness and compassion, you can proceed on to inner peace, forgiveness, love, acceptance of things that cannot be changed, and a deeper freedom for yourself and the loved ones directly affected by you.

Proverbs 19:8 says, "He who gets wisdom loves his own soul; he who cherishes understanding prospers." I believe that this is true regardless of how old we are, what problems we face, or what emotional crises may be holding us back.

I am from a Judeo-Christian background. As such, my values and beliefs will naturally be reflected in a thread that runs throughout this book. But I am not writing this to trick you into believing "my way." I simply want to be up front with you. This may be something you haven't always had in your life. In my research I noticed in adult children of divorce a strong tendency toward skepticism and mistrust of others. A common feeling for an ACD seems to be, "Everyone's got something to hide." This may come from a long ago experience with secrecy — muffled arguments in the night, bits of conversations overheard between parents or on the phone with their friends, relatives, or attorneys.

But I have nothing to hide. As you may know, the word psychiatry comes from two Greek words that mean "the study of the soul."[2] I hope that you enjoy this journey to look at the problems that often trouble the very souls of adult children of divorce and that you will find the information to be useful in your life.

The first and most pervasive aspect in many of the lives of ACDs is Dysfunctional Relationships. We'll look at the issues of relationships themselves first and then discuss the roots of problems that spring up in and around them throughout the rest of the book.

Adult Children of Divorce

-1-

Dealing with Dysfunctional Relationships

Millions of minor children are affected by their parents' divorces each year. The effects do not last just a few weeks or a few months, but they can have an impact for the rest of the children's lives. If we look at each nuclear family as a miniature "society," and consider the repercussions of disassembling each of these "societies" for those in the family and people close to them, and then magnify the ripple effects into the world, we can more easily see that the fabric of our "global village" is indeed being weakened.

The tears in the fabric, however, can be mended with love, patience, kindness, hope, and self-caring. Since they are not necessarily able to learn by the example of their parents, children of divorce may need help to learn how to have and maintain healthy relationships .

An extremely common trait among adult children of divorce today is codependency in some form or another. The prefix, co-, means "jointly, together." That would not seem to be a problem for an intimate relationship except that the healthier way to be is interdependent, not codependent. "Inter" means mutually dependent, or an interchangeable reliance on someone else for support. We can look at the difference between the two in this way: Codependent would be if one hand moves, a foot always does too. Interdependent means that the hand or foot may move without the other one moving—but chances are one is aware of the other.

Codependency occurs when one person says, "Jump!": and the other asks, "How high?" It happens when something another person is doing is destructive to himself and you, yet you enable him to continue the destruction by allowing or tolerating his behavior. You may associate codependency with relationships affected by alcohol or other drug use, but there are many "addictions" and other dysfunctions in relationships that do not involve such tangible evidence of destruction.

As a group, adult children of divorce exhibit other, more subtle signs of dysfunction in their relationships. And since relationships are such a big part of our lives, in this chapter we will look at several examples of dysfunction in order to see clearly how the significant life relationships of many ACDs may be affected.

The following subjects show up so often in the lives of ACDs struggling with dysfunctional relationship problems that a full chapter will be devoted to each of them:

1. Frantic Life Living
2. The Tendency to Extremes
3. Insecurity
4. The Great Need for Consistency
5. The Fear of Abandonment
6. Low Self-esteem
7. Loneliness
8. Physical Ailments and Emotional Drain
9. The Quest for Control

If you find yourself in the arms of, or in friendships with, people who seem to bring pain and conflict into your life whenever they're around, you are most likely involved in relationship patterns that are dysfunctional.

If you tolerate the abuse of others, then you are most certainly in dysfunctional relationships. If you cling to relationships because you're afraid nobody else will want you just as you are, then you plainly lean toward an addiction to unhealthy relationships.

If you feel it is "normal" to live with hostility and in crisis situations, then you most likely need professional help to begin to break the cycle of unhealthy relationship patterns.

There are nearly as many forms of dysfunction within relationships as there are relationships themselves. Let's look briefly at how dysfunctions can manifest themselves in relationships in unhealthy ways before we address each ACD problem in depth.

Tail-Chasing

Often, we spend so much energy cleaning up "messes" in unhealthy relationships that life becomes frantic, if only from trying to fit the normal needs of everyday life into schedules around the emotional and physical damage we contend with in dysfunctional relationships.

For example, Alice and Rob argue and debate some so-called problem nearly every day. They are addicted to the adrenaline rush of battle. Everything is a hassle—what they eat, where they hang a new painting, whether or not they will buy a new car, how they will manage their Christmas schedule.

In reality, both Alice and Rob have varying amounts of underlying hostilities and anger that were unintentionally transmitted to them via their parents. Alice and Rob were in elementary school when both sets of parents divorced. They unwittingly absorbed many of the tensions and conflicts they were exposed to (and became victims of) as children.

As adults, Alice and Rob are not aware that many of the problems they absorbed as children have become tributaries of resentment, bitterness, fear, and guilt. These seethe just beneath the surface of their consciousness. So they argue. They pick. They criticize. They ridicule. They re-circulate all the old hurts and it keeps them feeling alive—because that's what they learned from observing their parents.

Meanwhile, their patterns of relating keep them frantically shuffling through life. They fight. They go to work and can't do their jobs effectively because they're worried about the fight. They plan their emotional reunion. They make up. They remember the tasks they've left undone. They scramble to perform and meet their obligations. Then they fight and the vicious cycle begins again—they chase their tails.

Alice and Rob are addicted to their dysfunctional way of relating. This addiction destroys them insidiously. It can ruin peace in every area of their lives until those involved become convinced that all relationships are miserable. That's what they learned from watching their parents, and they subconsciously absorbed varying hostilities and angers at a young age and transmitted them into their own relationship.

A frightening aspect of this is that more than likely, whether Alice and Rob divorce or not, they will in turn transmit their unhealthy patterns onto their own children who may never know why they have a need to argue through their own relationships. Therefore, even if divorce is once or twice removed from the generations, its effects can march loudly on through time.

The next issue that often manifests itself in the dysfunctional relationships of adult children of divorce is a distorted sense of betrayal.

Learning to Betray

Divorcing parents often burden their children by literally teaching them how to betray their loved ones. They do this by expecting, even demanding, that their children take the side of one parent against the other. This commonly can even extend to the relationship kids have with relatives and friends of the family.

Cheryl remembers her mother forcing her to spy on her father during and after the couple's divorce. She was eleven when her parents split up.

"My mom would send me off to my dad's with a whole mental list of questions to answer for her: Was there another woman's robe in his closet? Did he mention getting a raise at work? Did he discuss any upcoming vacations?

"She grilled me for information each time I arrived home from a visit. And she also had the nerve to demand that I keep secrets from Dad, or lie to him. She'd say, 'Don't tell him I went away for the weekend. Tell him how poor we are and maybe he'll give us more money. Don't tell your dad you got in trouble at school last week or he'll blame me.'"

"Oh! How I hated those times!" Cheryl cries. It is not a coincidence that Cheryl's best friends and closest co-workers often ask her to cover up their mistakes, tell white lies for them, and to keep secrets from others for them.

Even though Cheryl detests lying, spying, and keeping secrets, this is a relating pattern she learned quite thoroughly and she does her "part" automatically. Before she even knows what's happened an incident is over.

This type of learned betrayal is extremely destructive and difficult for ACDs to work through. After all, parents are parents, and Cheryl had to be loyal to her mother's wishes because Cheryl was a child and she loved her mom! It became an ingrained response for Cheryl to cooperate with her mother's unethical manipulations. Cheryl couldn't betray her mom. If she did, her mother might leave her. Her father already had.

As an adult, Cheryl subconsciously relates the same way in her grown-up relationships. If a friend asks her to call in to work and tell the boss he's sick, it would be a betrayal to him if Cheryl didn't—and he may desert her!

Betrayal is a powerful issue because it works into the very essence of one's being. We grow up sensing that we are a product of our parents. If we betray our parents then we ultimately betray ourselves. If we betray ourselves, who do we have left?

Playing Both Ends against the Middle

Another tendency among ACDs involves loyalty to others when that loyalty may be undeserved, unhealthy, and even dangerous.

Very quickly during his parents' divorce, Phillip learned that loyalty and taking sides was a fine art to be learned if he was to make his way through the double dose of emotional quicksands he had to cope with at the same time—divorce and adolescence.

Often, to get his own way, he would side with the parent who would most likely grant him his wish. Phillip would carry out intricate plots to prove his "loyalty" to that parent and ultimately get his own way.

"One time I wanted to go on this camp-out. My mom said absolutely not because she suspected it was a big party—which it was. I thought the whole thing through very carefully. I knew my dad was real jealous of my mom's boyfriend. So, I called my dad up one night when Mom was gone. I just 'happened' to bring up the fact that her boyfriend had taken her to the fanciest restaurant in town and that they were going to drive to the lake in his Porsche afterward to see an outdoor concert that cost big bucks to get into.

"I knew my dad was struggling financially and that these were the right buttons to push. Then I paid my dad a few well-placed compliments about how great he was. Once I was sure he knew where my loyalties were, I casually mentioned having a few days off school the next week and that it would sure be nice to spend some time together.

"My dad fell for it completely. My mom thought it was great for me to go to my dad's the next week because she and her boyfriend wanted to go away. All I had to do with my dad was make a few strategic remarks that pitted him against Mom's boyfriend and I was on my way to the camp-out!"

Unfortunately, this dangerous loyalty-versus-betrayal game Phillip played as a kid spilled over into his adult life. Knowing how to feign his loyalty to others and elicit loyalty from them in return, has gotten him in jail for a fraudulent stock and embezzlement scheme that he orchestrated via a seemingly "loyal" relationship with his boss during his employment at an investment brokerage.

People go to all sorts of extremes to get their way, to feel more comfortable, or to be accepted and loved by others, largely because we instinctively strive to meet our basic, human needs. And we do what we have to do to survive.

Trying to Meet Our Basic Needs

Any of our everyday patterns of relating to others can become addictive and dysfunctional because our instincts are driving us to survive — even if we must use methods that we've learned which may be unhealthy. In his book, *God's Transforming Love*, Dr. Lloyd John Ogilvie tells us that our four generic and abiding needs are:

1. To be loved;
2. To feel forgiven;
3. To experience security;
4. To sense an adequate hope for the future.[1]

These needs often go unmet for members of divorcing families as they scramble to survive. Various forms of dysfunctional and addictive relationship patterns may begin from within the intense struggle to satisfy our deepest needs.

This is especially true for adult children of divorce because many have not had functional models of healthy relationships by those close to them over the long haul. They continue to relate to others in the only ways they know how.

Sandy became addicted to allowing people to boss her around because her four basic needs were not met consistently during her growing up years. When her husband demanded she do something unreasonable, she did it for fear he would leave her. If her employer placed outrageous expectations upon her, she exhausted herself to perform for fear of getting fired. If her girlfriends asked her to baby-sit their children at all times of the day and night, she did so because she certainly didn't want them to be angry with her. Sandy had learned to survive by doing the bidding of others in order to feel loved, secure, and accepted. Like so many ACDs, Sandy paid emotional blackmail dividends to others because this is how she got her basic needs met in her divorced family.

There are relationships where dysfunctions and addictions show themselves in the form of one spouse tolerating another's constant nagging or laziness; a friend who's constantly borrowing clothes or other personal items and not returning them; an employer who uses an ACD's vulnerable nature to further his/her own ends; or any number of unhealthy instances where emotional blackmail dividends are paid to meet basic, human needs.

The pressure you feel to "do anything to maintain the status quo" comes from learning to react according to the circumstances in ways that will allow you to survive in the least painful cocoon of existence. Sometimes this means to take part in a codependent network that revolves around the needs and behavior of a central character.

ACDs Can Become Like Tetherball Poles

Many adult children of divorce become the central characters in their own codependent family networks — or they play the lead, supporting roles. Like the tetherball poles on school playgrounds, ACDs stand while the others in their lives revolve around them in one way or another, trying to fulfill their needs and meet their demands. The others in the family can become like the tetherballs on the ends of ropes, wrapping themselves around the ACD in an effort to keep a certain amount of balance in their family networks.

ACDs often had to learn how to let life go on around them

like this all the while they struggled to meet their own basic needs because they were so overburdened due to their parents' divorces.

Pat's life is an almost constant state of nervous tension. She's so concerned with balancing each area of her life that she's overstressed to a great degree.

Pat is thirty-five. Her parents divorced when she was thirteen. As the oldest of four children, she immediately assumed the role of a caretaker in her family following the divorce.

Prior to the failure of her marriage, Pat's mother had never worked. When Pat's father left home, her mother took a job as a waitress in a local cafe. The position required long, irregular hours and Pat filled in the gaps at home by baby-sitting, supervising homework, cleaning house, making school lunches, sewing costumes for school plays, cooking dinners, doing laundry, and taking care of whatever else came along.

On weekends, when her friends were going to the movies, bowling, or attending athletic events at school, Pat was watching her younger brothers and little sister. Pat was extremely overburdened.

The family's life was essentially *out*-of-control. Throughout Pat's next five years at home, she absorbed much of the responsibility of raising herself and her siblings. Not only that, she also had to take care of her mother a lot of the time. Pat's mother was exhausted by the emotional, physical, and financial strains brought on by her divorce, going to work, and being a single parent. She became mentally unstable and Pat became the tetherball pole in her family.

Understandably, when Pat was finally on her own as a young adult, she determined that she alone would orchestrate her life. Unfortunately, she was so determined to have her needs met according to her design, that she planned her way into a lifestyle which was every bit as hectic and pressurized as her growing up was.

Pat married at age twenty, had two babies in the next four years, and started down a long path of codependent behavior that would eventually be her undoing.

She began by trying to control her husband, Loren. Loren was an easygoing man who was perfectly content to allow Pat to oversee their lives in the first months of marriage. He didn't feel any need to have a voice in how the household was run or what they did socially.

Pat was perfectly content because she felt in control — until their first Christmas together as a married couple. Loren mentioned casually one morning that it would be great to go "home" for the holidays as a married man.

Little did Loren know that he was hitting a double-wound with Pat. In the first place, her memories of Christmas from the time after her parents' divorce were horrendous. Her parents had always argued over who got the kids. Her father lavished material gifts on the children which her mother deeply resented. During the holiday season there was turmoil, depression, and bitterness for Pat throughout her teen years.

Pat completely overreacted and became very angry at Loren for even suggesting what to do for Christmas without consulting her. As the youngest member of a nuclear family, Loren was used to being "mothered," so he was more or less shocked into submission by Pat's intense reaction. He didn't mind making a loop around the tetherball pole.

For Christmas that first year, Pat and Loren stayed at home by themselves and watched television. Pat felt secure. Loren felt isolated.

By the time Pat and Loren's children were in elementary school Loren was only a shell of the young man he'd been when he was married. But Pat felt loved, secure, and accepted.

Now Pat ruled every part of their lives with an iron hand. When Pat wanted new wallpaper for the dining room, she got it. If Pat didn't want to attend Loren's parents' anniversary dinner, they didn't go. If Pat wanted to vacation, they vacationed. If she wanted to dine out, get a set of encyclopedias, or have sex, that's exactly what happened. The whole family was wrapped around the tetherball pole.

Pat was turning her children into little robots. They stuck exactly to the schedule Pat had for their lives. Any variation of the schedule, even an illness, unsettled Pat. To keep her central role, Pat was a volunteer teacher's aide in their classrooms for half the day for each child. She was their den mother for scouts and sat through every piano lesson or baseball practice they had.

When Pat's mother became ill, Pat moved her into the spare bedroom in her home. Pat controlled everything from what her mother ate to what television programs she watched.

When Pat's siblings suggested that taking on the care of their mother was too much for Pat and Loren's family, Pat balked angrily. She wanted to know if they were trying to insinuate that she wasn't doing a good enough job. She railed at them bitterly that she'd always been the one to take care of all of them, including their mother, and she could handle it just fine—with no thanks to them.

Behind her back both her family and Loren's called Pat, "The Colonel." She was so incessant and demanding that it was easier to revolve around her when in her presence and then get away from her as quickly as possible.

Pat felt comfortable in this cocoon of codependency. Unfortunately, Pat couldn't maintain this kind of existence forever. Recently she had to have surgery for bleeding ulcers and was bedridden for a time according to doctor's orders.

Pat's doctor told her she must rest in bed for at least three weeks and not do a full day's activities for at least six. Then she is to slow down from her normal pace by at least half. He's informed Pat that if she continues to put herself under so much strain, trying to do everything for everybody, she's going to kill herself.

Pat's confinement is actually a big relief to Loren, the kids, the kids' teachers, Pat's mother, and all their relatives. But it's driving Pat crazy. While Loren is thrilled simply to decide what he'll take to work for lunch, Pat is certain he'll take only junk food. As the kids delight in choosing their own clothes for a day, Pat is fussing over the fact that this or that doesn't match quite right. Nothing is done well enough by Pat's standards. The tetherball is unwinding from the pole and not revolving for now.

According to Pat, the laundry is turning gray, the kitchen floor is grimy, and her mother isn't getting a balanced diet. Pat is going wild and everyone around her is inwardly glad to have a chance to escape her clutches.

The relationships in Pat's life are all dysfunctional to some degree because they all revolve around her in one way or another. Pat's neurotic influence is similar to a puppeteer pulling the strings of a marionette. But she doesn't even know it. She really believes that the significant people in her life can't get along without her. To some twisted extent they believe this also or they would not tolerate her tyranny. They are codependents — doing what they think are the right things for the right reasons when all the while they are enabling Pat to destroy herself and them!

Part of this Pat learned from her adolescent experience, and part of her demands that she have control in order for her to survive emotionally. She's really a very frightened little girl with a Piggy-Back Child squeezing around her neck.

People cannot know that they are addicted to dysfunctional relationships unless they know how to recognize healthy, functional ones. Let's look at how healthy relationships work.

Management: Defining Healthy Relationships

In healthy relationships people (in pairs or a network) give, take, interact, and enjoy one another *comfortably*. Healthy relationships are those in which people are interdependent on one another. It's sort of like lacing your fingers together as if to pray — your hands intertwine comfortably, but when you take them apart each hand can function just fine on its own.

In a network of people, such as a family, corporation, or community, the same thing holds true, only on a bigger scale. The network should not always revolve around the same person's moods, whims, and needs!

Healthy relationships come into and go out of focus over a period of time. One person in a network may need all eyes on him during a time of grieving or celebrating. Later, another person's needs become sharply visible and the first one is healthy enough to be able to fade softly into the background.

Healthy relationships diffuse into the worlds in which the people live. A wife has a career. A husband has a career. Together they have each other, their children, their household and friends. She has her extended family, he has his, and they also share these. She has her own friends, he has his. If their private relationship is healthy, chances are their other relationships will be in balance also, most of the time.

Healthy relationships are like a well-choreographed dance routine. If the routine is made for more than one person, it will most likely bomb if done by a solitary dancer. But it will come to life and be highly successful if each person does his or her part. This is not to say that healthy relationships don't have problems, because they do! Conflict is very much a part of healthy relationships.

All Healthy Relationships Have Conflict

For adult children of divorce, conflict can be a very frightening and confusing thing. But it is a normal part of every healthy relationship! All healthy relationships have ups, downs, problems, and pockets of neuroses. Conflict can be the outgrowth of dealing with these. The friction of conflict helps an already healthy relationship become better.

Dan Thorne, a marriage, family, and child counselor at the Miller Psychological Center in Orange, California, says, "Being a good couple does not mean never disagreeing. Being a good couple means being able to disagree."[2]

Often, adult children of divorce have seen far too many examples of destructive conflict. Healthy marriages do not break up. And when an unhealthy marriage is dissolved there is commonly an inability on the part of the adults who are divorcing to disagree in a healthy way.

Many ACDs recall being witness to bitter arguments, name-calling, physical violence, acute withdrawal, vicious court battles, malicious behavior, and financial feuds.

These kinds of unhealthy conflicts do not lend themselves to a kindly view of disagreeing with others. Nor do they encourage feeling secure in intimate relationships with others. If adult children of divorce haven't had healthy examples of conflict and haven't seen satisfactory resolution of disagreements, they're not going to know automatically how to deal with differences in relationships. Therefore, they often either try to avoid conflict altogether, which eliminates healthy relationships, or panic when confronted with conflict, which discourages healthy relationships. It can be a difficult cycle to break.

However, there are steps that can be taken to break *all* of the troubling cycles that have been mentioned. The same process applies to each and begins with balancing or eliminating the dysfunctional relationships in your life. The following steps can be taken toward breaking each dysfunctional cycle and having healthier relationships:

1. Become aware that there are problems in your life and of what behavior you have in which you need to make some changes.

2. Modify and eventually stop destructive behaviors with which you are involved.

3. Get whatever help you need to gain knowledge, wisdom, and understanding of yourself and your past. Let go of unhealthy behavior.

4. Apply the helps, knowledge, wisdom, and understanding to your life to change your behavior patterns. Your emotions will follow suit. You can't change the way the engine of a train goes and not have the caboose follow along.

5. Allow yourself joy!

The giving and taking of healthy relationships is not usually a consistent, fifty-fifty deal. You may need to be first! You may need to take control of your life and behavior. You may need to accept that the significant people in your life will be threatened by changes in you. But believe that there are people who can and will come into your life who are good for you and God *will* put them there.

Don't deny conflict in your relationships. Conflict is often the impetus for change and growth. It is the flame which cooks the ingredients that are already in the pot!

Next, do the following exercise to evaluate the significant relationships in your life to see if they may be healthy or have some degree of dysfunction.

EXERCISE: EVALUATING YOUR RELATIONSHIPS

Get paper and pen. Make the following headings at the top of a page:

WHO   INITIAL FEELING   ACTION   END FEELING

Now sit quietly by yourself. Imagine for a moment that you are sitting in your favorite spot. Perhaps you are on a grassy hillside, at a beach, in a garden, at a restaurant, in a soft chair, or anywhere you'd really love to be.

Now imagine the first person who comes to mind, happening upon you in your favorite place. Mentally consider the answers to the following questions:

1. How did you feel when you saw this person? Delighted? Shocked? Sad? Resentful?

2. Did you want this person to stay with you or leave you to yourself? Did you want the person to stay and talk with you or to remain silent?

3. Why is this person the first one to come to mind? Is he/she someone with whom you feel particularly safe? Are you having problems with him/her? Is it a person you spend a lot of time with? Someone with whom you wish you could spend more time?

4. As the person stays, or after he/she leaves, do you feel better than you did before you first saw him/her in your favorite spot? Worse? Indifferent? Upset? At peace?

5. Do you wish this person hadn't come? Are you happy that he/she did?

6. Are there things you would like or need to discuss with this person? Is this person living or dead?

Take the collective answers to your questions and write them in your own personal shorthand under the headings you wrote at the top of the page.

Now, go through these same steps with other people, one a time—let each person come upon you in your favorite place in the same way. Ask yourself the questions with each encounter. Chart your answers under the headings. Now see if any patterns have evolved:

1. Are the people you meet all loved ones?
2. People it is easy for you to be with?
3. People toward whom you have ill feelings?
4. People who make you nervous?
5. People from your past?
6. "Everyday" people you see at work, during errands, etc.?
7. Are they mostly people you fantasize about, such as movie stars?

If there is a pattern, then try to see what it is and consider why it looks this way. For instance, if these people are loved ones with whom you feel safe and secure, do you simply get a warm, happy feeling to think about them? Or do you feel a need to be protected by them?

If the people who happened upon you are all people you wanted to leave you alone, ask yourself why.

Did only one person come to mind when you were imagining? Do you have a particularly strained relationship with this person right now? Did only a group of people come to you in your favorite spot?

For every person you imagined—whether your parents, stepparents, spouse, children, boss, teacher, neighbor, or co-worker—consider whether or not your life revolves around that person. If so, how?

Are all your life decisions affected by what your parents or in-laws will think? Does a stepparent mandate how you live? Does your spouse's behavior dictate the mood of your whole household all the time? If your life revolves around any one person in a relationship, then that relationship is dysfunctional to some degree.

If you see or feel indications of dysfunction, consider getting advice or seeking professional help to delve into the situation further. Also, bear in mind that most healthy relationships do have pockets of dysfunctional areas — all of life is one large growth process!

One of the outward symptoms of a life troubled by dysfunction, or the Piggy-Back Children who come into adulthood with those from divorced families, is frantic life living. In chapter 2 we will look at "Frantic Life Livers" and consider why they do live at such an extremely hectic pace.

-2-

Keeping Up the Pace

We're all too busy these days, it seems. There are so many places to go, people to see, and things to do that it is common to feel that life may spin out of control at any moment. We often dash from home to work to home, and run circles around ourselves trying to keep up sound relationships with our spouses, children, co-workers, friends, relatives, and selves. Life in the '80s has left many of us longing for a saner pace in the '90s.

For adult children of divorce in our society, keeping up a frantic life's pace can create such pressure that it is near torment compared to the "normal" amount of "hectic." And ACDs have been coping with this push for nearly a generation.

For the most part, the jury's still deliberating about how divorce affects children long-term. Only now do we have a group of ACDs large enough to see what problems are most common to them. There are few resources to tell us what's going on. But as the jury reaches a verdict, time management and frantic living are among the most prominent and insidious complications in the lives of ACDs. Research shows that "Frantic Life Livers" exhibit their behavior in three ways:

1. She fills every waking moment of her life with activity because she watched her divorced parents struggle from morning until late night to meet the demands brought on by pulling a family apart—maintaining self, home, children, work, finances, new relationships as well as pre-existing ones. It has become "natural" for this adult to run, run, run because that was the example she had while growing up.

2. He fills his time to overflowing because, somewhere deep inside, he feels that if he's good enough, he will be loved and approved of—finally. He may be operating from a "swivel base reaction" to his parents' divorce. As a child he may have wanted his parents to get back together so badly that he "swivelled" his behavior sporadically in attempts to try to be "good enough" so his parents would remarry. As he grew up, this behavior gained momentum, even took on a life of its own. Now the adult just keeps reacting from the same swivel base—his life is absolutely frantic!

3. He fills up every waking minute because, if he doesn't, he may accidentally bump into his own true emotions. As a child he learned to keep busy to avoid the emotional realities he was living with at home. His feelings may have been pushed away because his parents' feelings were top priority. So he "got busy" to escape his pain. As an adult he still stays busy to distance himself from painful emotions.

These three types of frantic life livers tend to go faster and faster until some kind of physical or emotional crisis forces him/her to *stop!* At this point, it is important to their healing that they seek help from reliable, sensitive, and perceptive sources, such as a medical doctor who's known them for a long while, a counselor who is well aware of the undercurrents that can often direct external lifestyles, a pastor who is trained to counsel delicate issues, or a friend who is familiar with an ACD's background.

An ACD may be one pure type of frantic life liver; more likely, he lives a too-frantic pace for a combination of all three reasons. Let's look in on the internal workings of someone who exemplifies all three kinds of frantic life living.

Too Busy Is "Normal"

Laura Mitchell had been having a recurring nightmare for several weeks. In it, she was being chased by a crowd of people down the sidewalk of a city street. The crowd included her husband, children, and parents. Though she didn't know why they were chasing her in the dream, she kept running until she couldn't go one step farther. At this point she always woke up in a sweat, her heart pounding and her head throbbing.

The repeating dream really bothered Laura. She couldn't think of a reason why she'd be haunted by any deep-seated emotional problem that would prompt such a seemingly simple nightmare. But it was wearing her out! So, she made an appointment with her family physician, Dr. Fullbrook.

Laura had first seen Dr. Fullbrook as a ten-year-old girl with an awful case of the mumps. He'd been new in the medical clinic then and the only doctor who could see her that particular day. But a rapport with Laura's mother was immediately struck and Dr. Fullbrook had been the family's doctor for more than thirty years. In fact, he was now nearing retirement and Laura's youngest child would enter high school in the fall. Dr. Fullbrook had been through many ups and downs with Laura. He was there when her parents divorced as she was about to turn twelve. He'd delivered her two daughters into the world, and given them their mumps vaccinations.

After Laura related her dream to the doctor, he looked at her closely. Just telling him about it appeared to agitate her. He was glad that this was his last appointment of the day and he had the time to talk with her.

"Well, Laura," he said gently, "let's look at the things we know about you and see if they'll tell us something we *don't* know. Then we can try to put the two sides together and figure out why you're being pestered with this dream."

Laura nodded. She almost felt silly now—it was only a dream. She shouldn't have been so quick to think she needed help with something so simple!

Thankfully, Dr. Fullbrook knew of Laura's tendency to negate her own needs and brought up a first point that helped to eliminate her embarrassment. "Now, Laura, we know that you have a habit of pushing your own needs off and convincing yourself that they're not important. Can you think of anything that happened about the same time you began having this dream that may be related in some way?"

Laura thought back to the first night she woke up in a panic from being chased. It had been just before her oldest daughter's prom. Laura had been staying up late sewing dresses; she was busy helping on the refreshment committee, cleaning the house for a party after the dance, and putting centerpieces together for the banquet tables. Laura remembered the first dream because it was on an evening when she woke up to find her daughter and a boyfriend necking on the family room sofa.

This had upset Laura terribly because she'd always felt comfortable going to bed and leaving her daughter with friends or a date to visit privately or watch movies. But after this incident, Laura felt that she needed to be a "police-mom" and stay awake until all guests were gone for the night.

Laura explained all this to Dr. Fullbrook. He considered her story for a few moments and then asked slowly, "What else has been happening in the last couple of months?"

Laura tilted her head to one side, thinking. She noticed the broad green leaves on the maple tree outside Dr. Fullbrook's office window. Summertime was always a pressure-packed season for Laura—keeping up with work, the house, increased social demands, and having the kids running in and out at odd, unscheduled times. Just coping was a struggle.

She looked back at Dr. Fullbrook, "Hmm. What hasn't been happening would be a better question. Once I got through the prom, then I had eighth grade graduation to deal with for our younger daughter. My husband's company took a nose dive on the stock market so he's been moody and worried. My mom's been calling me every morning to tell me about a new ache she has and what her neighbors are doing. My boss was promoted so I'm learning to relate to his replacement. We're remodeling a bathroom so there are workers at the house all week. And the girls are home off and on every day and don't pick up after themselves so I have to clean first thing each day when I get home from work. I joined the health club to try to get in 'swimsuit shape' for our annual Labor Day BBQ at the lake, and an old friend from high school is coming to visit for a week in several days so I'm getting ready for that."

Dr. Fullbrook watched Laura carefully as she talked. Her eyes widened, she grew more tense, and her breathing quickened noticeably. He smiled at her with a knowing nod, "Uff! It exhausts me just hearing about the pace you're trying to keep up!

"Let's stop and consider something for a moment. We've already mentioned that you tend to push your own needs aside to meet those of others. Now, we know from your past that you also have a tendency to fill your schedule so full that it's almost impossible to live with. It appears to me that you are in an overload position again, Laura. What do you think?"

"Certainly I would agree that I'm overloaded, Dr. Fullbrook. But it's all with regular life stuff. Nobody can avoid the normal responsibilities of marriage, parenting, and work!"

"No, that's right," Dr. Fullbrook agreed. "However, I know your personality too well to let you get by with writing this dream off to simply an exception to the rule or as a result of the 'normal' responsibilities of a family. Laura, you've overloaded yourself with commitments since you were a teenager!

"It wasn't enough to be an A-student, you had to be a cheerleader, on the debate team, in speech contests, and in every dramatic, musical, or student governing activity that was available. Remember when your girls were in elementary school and you were room mother to both their classes?

"Yes, life is very busy these days with two-worker families, more opportunities for involvement, and more demands to meet. But you have a longstanding pattern of overextending, Laura. Can you think of any reasons why?"

Laura's eyes lit up with an idea. She looked at Dr. Fullbrook with excitement, "You know, Doctor, we've both mentioned the 'normal' responsibilities of marriage and family life, and you brought up my being so busy ever since I was a teenager. Look at the parallels.

"I filled my schedule too full within several months of my parents' divorce—maybe overloaded is *normal for me!*

"Remember how my mom went back to work after the divorce? Well, I can still see her in the kitchen in the morning when I'd get up—already fixing lunches, baking cookies for a school party, and doing her bookwork. I can recall her just sitting down to fold clothes, look over our school papers, and answer letters as we kids were getting ready for bed.

"Regardless of the divorce and of the fact that Mom's whole life changed, she still tried to keep up the same responsibilities and fulfill the same obligations as before! To her, getting up at 4:30 A.M. and going to bed near midnight became *normal*. I grew up thinking that also!"

Dr. Fullbrook grinned, "What a delightful realization, Laura! My initial instinct tells me that you're right! Like the old saying goes, 'Children learn what they live.' And it is also in keeping with your pushing your own needs aside. Surely your mother also did this in keeping up with the demands made upon her as a single, working parent running an entire household."

Dr. Fullbrook continued, "Okay, so we can see clearly where you picked up the habits of filling your life with too many frantic days. How do you think this may correlate to your dream?"

Laura was stumped. She didn't see any reason why she

would repeatedly dream that a whole crowd of people, including her family, would be chasing her—running her into a frenzy. But it was very obvious to Dr. Fullbrook and he said so. "I think you've had all you can take, Laura! All the committees, requests for your time, and demands for your attention are just too much for you to bear anymore. And those who have expectations for you are the primary faces in the crowd—your husband, children, and mother!

"Now I'm not saying it's their fault you're overloaded. They simply expect of you what you'll give—kind of like spilled water will fill in the spaces available to it. You've allowed your family free rein with your time and talents over the years, and they fill up every space you make available to them!"

Laura looked perplexed. "Are you saying I want to literally run away from my family?"

"No, not literally," Dr. Fullbrook answered. "But, I think perhaps you do want to escape some of the demands they're making on you. Perhaps you resent them for continually asking more of you when you think they should know and see how busy you already are."

"I can go that one, for sure," Laura responded. "It really irks me that my mother calls me in the early mornings to fuss and complain. After all, she knows I'm getting ready for work then. And it really, really irritates me that the girls won't pick up after themselves in these summer months!"

Performing Well Enough to Earn Love and Approval

Dr. Fullbrook looked Laura directly in the eyes and asked, "Why don't you ask your mother to call you at other times of the day, or leave your daughters lists of things to do around the house while you're gone at work?"

"I've tried that!" Laura said in exasperation. "They don't pay any attention—and besides, it's easier just to put up with Mom or do the housework than it is to fight the flow!"

"What flow?" Dr. Fullbrook prodded.

Laura hesitated before saying, "The flow of family, I guess."

"Kind of like the flow of the crowd in your dream?" Dr. Fullbrook was quick to make the connection.

Laura seemed taken aback. "Why! Yes! I suppose so. It's easier for me to run in the same direction they're going and try to stay ahead of the pack than it is to try to turn around and move against the flow."

"Laura," Dr. Fullbrook put his words together slowly, "what do you think would happen if you did go against the flow?"

Laura unconsciously bit at her bottom lip. "I don't know for sure. Maybe I'd be bumped and shoved in the crowd."

"And if you were, say pushed from side to side and poked with a few elbows as you struggled against the crowd, would that be so terrible?"

"Yes!" Laura said with certainty.

"Why?" the kindly doctor asked.

"Because," Laura searched her mind quickly for an answer. "Because it would hurt."

"I see," Dr. Fullbrook said. "And how would it hurt?"

Simply thinking about going against the flow of her family in a dream, a pretend situation, was making Laura very nervous. The Piggy-Back Child was pulling on her desperately. Laura put an index finger to the spot where she was biting her bottom lip. Dr. Fullbrook could see she was pressing hard because the knuckle turned white. Laura's eyes looked pained as she spoke, "It would hurt by pushing me in directions I don't want to go."

"And what directions do you mean?"

"Oh! I don't know!" Laura exclaimed. "I just don't want to make any waves by even trying to go against the flow!"

"Laura," Dr. Fullbrook inquired, "what makes you think that by asking your mother to call you at times that are convenient for you, or by expecting your daughters to help around the house, you are going against the flow?"

"Because," Laura's voice became shrill, "whenever I ask

anyone in the family to do anything they get upset with me!"

A light of understanding flashed in Dr. Fullbrook's mind. He tipped back in his chair and said with confidence, "What you're trying to say is that if you do enough 'right' things for your family members then they will approve of and appreciate you. In essence, you're saying you feel a need to earn their love — if you're good enough they will love you."

Laura's chin quivered. Dr. Fullbrook could see he'd hit on target. He leaned across his desk and held out his hands to Laura. She placed her small fists in Dr. Fullbrook's large, open palms and he wrapped his strong fingers around her hands with a comforting pressure.

"Laura, I must be perfectly blunt with you," he said softly. "I believe that what you're really telling me is that you are running yourself to death, trying to do all the right things at the right times and for all the right reasons so that your family will love and approve of you — not reject you. I think you are scared silly to think that if you confront those you love with your own needs and desires they will turn their backs on you like — "

"Stop!" Laura cried. She pulled her hands from Dr. Fullbrook's grasp and slumped back into her seat. "I know what you're going to say — like my dad did!"

Dr. Fullbrook was not going to lose the opportunity opening up before him. "Is that true, Laura? Is it true that deep inside you feel like your dad left home because you weren't good enough and your other loved ones may leave you too if you don't behave the way they expect you to, or if you place any demands on them?"

Laura's body crumpled in her chair. She appeared to be the small, hurting Piggy-Back Child that had haunted her into adulthood — ever since the little girl's daddy had left home and the girl absorbed the belief that if only she had been a "good enough" daughter her daddy would have stayed within the family.

Tears washed down Laura's cheeks as she answered, "Yes, Dr. Fullbrook. Yes, that is true. But honestly, until this very moment I did not realize it!"

"It's all right, Laura," Dr. Fullbrook soothed. "There are

many, many things we all have that prompt us to behave in ways we don't understand. The key is that once we are aware of them and move toward understanding, then we can begin to make choices that are healthier and better for us!"

Laura's shoulders heaved and her eyes puffed up as she sobbed out years worth of pent-up fears and misguided self-expectations. Dr. Fullbrook let her cry and respected her dignity by keeping silent until he could see Laura's adult person overcome the jolt her Piggy-Back Child had given with helpless little girl emotions.

"I'm sorry, Doctor," Laura hiccupped as she took the box of tissue Dr. Fullbrook offered her. "I'm so shocked at all this — the dream, the automatic, frantic pace I've been living, and then to think that much of it also comes from a fear of being rejected by my loved ones — it's just overwhelming!"

"Of course it is, Laura," Dr. Fullbrook said compassionately, "and there is one more angle that we should look at before we wrap up this appointment."

Laura looked somewhat alarmed as she thought of considering more emotional aspects of what her seemingly simple nightmare meant.

Bumping into Yourself Accidentally

"It's okay, Laura," Dr. Fullbrook assured. "This won't be nearly so painful. You've actually already stumbled onto what I want to bring up — we just need to put it into words."

Laura nodded her permission to proceed and Dr. Fullbrook accepted.

"Let's consider for a few moments what we have come through today. Deep inside you there has been a force directing your life automatically. This force is actually threefold in the way it affects you as an adult.

"*First*, the force is learned — you learned how to be busier than is healthy for you by watching your mother frantically pushing her own needs aside, trying to keep up with the many needs of her family after a traumatic divorce.

"*Second*, the force is misguided—you've lived with an erroneous fear of being rejected if you weren't 'good enough' for your loved ones to approve of and stay with.

"*Third*, the force is bruised—you've repressed your negative, fearful emotions for so long that you fill up every waking moment with activities so that you won't risk bumping into your threatening, negative feelings accidentally."

As Dr. Fullbrook paused, Laura asked him quizzically, "What is the force, Doctor?"

"Ah, Laura, you truly are delightful! You know just what questions to ask. The force, my dear, is the frightened, confused, and lonely little girl who's ridden with you piggy-back ever since her parents were divorced!

"You know, Laura, when you break a soft, chocolate chip cookie—warm from the oven—in half, it rarely comes apart with even edges. Generally, the sides are jagged and rough. It's the same with pulling a family apart—there are many rough edges to deal with. We're beginning to cope with three reasons for one of your rough edges today."

"Hmm." Laura thought for a few seconds, "And why would I be afraid to risk bumping into myself accidentally?"

"Well, let me answer with another question. Do you have negative feelings toward members of your family that you don't necessarily admit, face up to, and deal with?"

"Uh-oh," Laura rolled her eyes toward the ceiling, "I feel another 'dream meaning' coming on! What do you think the answer to your question is?"

"I can't answer because I don't live inside your heart. But I do know you mentioned resenting your mother's phone calls and your daughters' not helping around the house. That may be a good place for us to start searching for feelings that may go deeper or be more powerful," Dr. Fullbrook suggested.

"Hmm," Laura pondered sincerely, "I think I see what you mean. There are things rattling around inside me that I'm not consciously aware of right now, and my little girl piggy-backs with me and pinches or pulls when the feelings get too close."

"Exactly!" Dr. Fullbrook said. "And tell me if you see a connection with your dream."

"Yes, I think there is. I think all three elements you mentioned are present in my dream. I feel that running away from the crowd with my family members in it means that:

"1. I am struggling to keep up an unhealthy pace that's become automatic to me because it's how I learned to be from watching my mom.

"2. I am running from, but going in the same direction as, my family because I don't want to make any emotional waves by *not* keeping up the frantic pace of my life and risking their rejection.

"3. Also, I am running away because I don't want to take the chance that I might 'bump into my own emotions' and have to face negative feelings or conflicts with my family if my feelings require confrontation."

"I agree completely!" Dr. Fullbrook smiled emphatically. "I think you've come a long way toward eliminating your middle-of-the-night encounters with panic today, Laura! What say I send you on your way today and we make another appointment for next week at this time? You can be thinking of any underground feelings that may try to surface now that you're aware they're probably lurking around. When you come next week we'll talk about more healthy ways you can manage your life. Who knows? Maybe you'll dream a new dream this week!"

Laura grinned broadly. She was immensely relieved to have explored such a tremendous amount of emotional ground about herself with Dr. Fullbrook in just a short time.

MANAGEMENT: CONSIDERING WHY YOU RUSH

When Laura arrived at Dr. Fullbrook's office the next week she could hardly wait her turn to see him. She had purposely made her appointment at the end of his day again so they would have plenty of time. She had hardly sat down in the chair opposite him before she began bubbling over with news of the exciting week she'd had.

"Oh! Dr. Fullbrook! You won't believe it! I've had such a great week!" Laura burst out. "Well, not all of it was great," she said, "but the end results were!"

"Really?" Dr. Fullbrook smiled, "Tell me, by all means."

"First, I haven't had my nightmare once! I've slept all night, every night, since I saw you last week. Second, I've realized several things I've been feeling but that I didn't allow to surface before."

"Such as?" Dr. Fullbrook asked.

"Several things about my husband," Laura said plainly. "Like I've been resenting him because he's allowed me to take on such a load while he grapples with the problems at his company. Granted, he's having a tough time since they took their dive on the market, but I've been dealing with my transition at work too, and I've still kept up my end of things plus taking on his. I deal with all the household chores, the girls, my own work, the contractor who's remodeling the bathroom, and anything else that crops up. Anyway, I was relieved just to become aware that I have the resentments at all.

"It also dawned on me that I'm not only feeling inconvenienced by my mother's daily phone calls in the morning, but I'm actually angry at her for not paying more attention to my needs. Do you think that may be a leftover from the divorce?"

"Could be," Dr. Fullbrook acknowledged. "I am very happy that you are making such clear discoveries about your feelings. Can you tell me what you may do with or about your awareness to make life a little easier on yourself?"

At this point, Laura's face fell. "*Do*?" she questioned. "I don't know. I guess I was so happy to be able to think my feelings consciously I didn't anticipate doing anything about them."

"Perfectly normal," Dr. Fullbrook responded cheerily. "Most people react to newfound knowledge of themselves like that. But the key to real life change, Laura, is going to come when you choose to manage your time and organize yourself."

Laura looked somewhat uneasy. She squirmed in her chair and asked tentatively, "What do you mean, choose?"

"Relax, Laura," Dr. Fullbrook advised. "It's nothing so painful you need to worry! Let's take each area of your frantic life-pace and brainstorm ways to manage:

"1. The things you do automatically from having observed your mother juggling so many demands — pushing her own needs aside. What are some things you can think of to do that may help break the pattern?"

Laura thought for a few moments before responding, "I can start practicing at saying no to some of the people who ask me to take on committees and to do other extracurricular things."

"Excellent!" Dr. Fullbrook praised. "What else?"

"I can stop piling new projects on myself and eliminate as many of my present ones as possible."

"Such as?"

"Such as not taking on a bathroom remodeling unless life is less hectic at work for my husband and me. And maybe asking my old high school friend to visit another time."

"Uh-huh!" Dr. Fullbrook clapped his hands together enthusiastically. "You are on the right track, Laura!"

"Actually, I know intellectually that I could ask my friend to come another time but emotionally I know I won't — I wouldn't want to hurt her feelings!" Laura looked at Dr. Fullbrook sheepishly.

He responded graciously, "That's okay. Sometime your awareness of what's healthy for you will spill over into your actions.

"There's another suggestion I'd like to add to your superb thoughts. I can't imagine you feeling comfortable with this type of thing yet, but it's an essential ingredient for mental health. That is for you to schedule yourself time every single day to do absolutely nothing but be in your own company!"

"Ha!" Laura was incredulous. "I'd have to stay up until two in the morning to do that, and then I'd risk one of the girls waking up, finding me, and wanting to chat!"

"I'm serious, Laura." Dr. Fullbrook pressed. "You'd be surprised at how wonderful it is to schedule time to do nothing and follow through on it! Promise me you'll try."

Laura shrugged her shoulders, "Okay. I'll write it on my list and try it for 15–20 minutes a day."

"Great!" Dr. Fullbrook said with hearty approval. "Now, let's move on to the second area of management:

"2. The things you've been doing because of a subconscious belief that if you're good enough, busy enough, or have done enough you'll keep hold of the love and approval of your family members — then they won't reject you. Any ideas about how you could handle this area?"

Laura was a little more reserved when she answered this question, "I've been thinking about that a lot this week. I was remembering back to when Mom and Dad got divorced. Their love and approval meant everything to me. I wanted them to think highly of me so badly that I did get involved in every activity you said last week. The more I thought about my growing up and how our home life changed, the more I wondered about the fact that I never really did feel the approval I sought. Especially from my dad. And you know, he's dead now. I feel like maybe the pace of my life got even more frantic after his death. I don't know, maybe I'm still trying to get his approval in some strange way."

"Could be," Dr. Fullbrook agreed. "And I know that the issue of earning love and approval can be a real stickler for religious reasons sometimes."

Laura was quick to pick up this thread. "Yes! I've thought of that this week too. Where was God when my parents divorced? Did He abandon our family because He disapproves of divorce? Maybe it's His love and approval I'm ultimately trying to 'earn.'"

It was Dr. Fullbrook's turn to contemplate. Cautiously he said, "I know that no matter how painful the time of your parents' divorce was, God was there, and to this day He loves you just exactly the way you are! Let me look something up."

Dr. Fullbrook pulled open one of the top drawers of his desk and pulled out a worn, leatherbound Bible. Looking in the back, he quickly found what he was looking for and leafed through pages with the speed of familiarity.

"Ah! Here's a verse I want. In Hebrews 13:5 God says, 'Never will I leave you; never will I forsake you.' Never means *never*, Laura, regardless of the circumstances.

"Now, let me look up one more verse." Dr. Fullbrook deftly turned through his Bible again. When he found what he was looking for he smiled warmly and said, "Here, in Galatians 2:16, it tells us, 'Know that a man is not justified by observing the law, but by faith in Jesus Christ.' That tells me I cannot work my way to heaven or earn God's love and approval by doing all the 'right' things according to the rules."

Laura nodded appreciatively, "That helps a great deal, Doctor. I really should pay more attention to my faith, I suppose."

Dr. Fullbrook looked a little surprised, "I don't think there are any 'shoulds' involved, Laura; I think we have free will precisely so we can make that choice without feeling any duress. If you desire to develop a closer relationship with God, then you may want to use the time you're going to schedule to 'do nothing' to read in the Bible or a devotional book you're comfortable with."

"That's a good idea," Laura agreed. "And with my family or any other relationships where I find myself behaving to get love or approval, I can begin trying out new patterns of relating."

"Yes. Can you think of any examples of how that may happen?"

Laura scanned memories of her experiences with family, friends, and co-workers in recent weeks. She thought of three incidents when she acted the way she felt others wanted her to, versus how she would otherwise have chosen to behave.

"Well, last week my new boss wanted me to stay late at work. I wanted to impress him as a 'good' assistant so I stayed. In reality, it made me late for an open house at school and the whole family was affected. I could have explained the situation to him and told him that I don't approve of working past office hours except in extraordinary circumstances because I have other obligations."

"Wonderful!" Dr. Fullbrook encouraged.

"And there are two other things that come to mind off the top of my head. One is that several days ago my husband made it a point to let me know I'd fallen down in the baking department at home. He's grown accustomed to having cakes and cookies around all the time. That evening I stayed up late and baked muffins so they were there for him in the morning. Instead, I should have replied that I haven't had the energy or desire to bake lately with the transitions we're both going through at work and the remodeling going on at home.

"The last thing I thought of was a few weeks ago I let my oldest daughter go to a party I instinctively felt meant trouble. But I didn't want us to argue about why I didn't want her to go, so I allowed it. Sure enough, when she came home she said there'd been a group of high school boys there fighting and disturbing the neighbors. The police came to break it up.

"From now on I'll try to follow my instincts more. I think it's more vital that I'm a parent to my daughters now than a friendly pal."

"I couldn't agree with you more!" Dr. Fullbrook replied, "I think your thoughts are splendid on all three circumstances! I believe we can move on to the third aspect of frantic life-living:

"3. Facing the fact that you have negative feelings toward others that will come out somehow, some way, some day! Whether your attitude becomes bitter or you are forced to deal with an uncomfortable, recurring dream, it is very important to risk bumping into your own emotions! Any suggestions on how you can deal with this?"

Laura held up empty hands, "Other than realizing that filling up my days and nights with family, social, community, and church obligations won't make my resentments go away, I'm at a loss!"

"Well, I'd say that realization alone is an excellent gain!" Dr. Fullbrook said as he thumped his hands onto the arms of his chair. "I have one suggestion to help get you started in facing your negative feelings. It will help you get more comfortable with them. Get a notebook. Each day write down in your notebook how you honestly feel about the people you interacted with the day before —

if you're a morning person—or that day if you like to stay up late. This will be your *'honest time'* notebook. You can hide it or lock it up or destroy each page after you've written and considered it if you want. But be sure you do this! Take the time to look at how you truly feel about what's going on in your life day-by-day. This will help you get and stay in touch with your feelings."

Laura thought this was an excellent idea for someone like herself. She felt very hopeful about her new self-awareness, the techniques she'd been discussing with Dr. Fullbrook on how to best manage her frantic living habits in healthier ways and organizing her time better.

Laura thanked Dr. Fullbrook for his insight and support. He assured her that he would be there for her if she needed further help. They parted with an affectionate hug and Laura was off on a new journey to live more freely from the self-imposed demands she'd made on herself, turning her into a frantic life liver!

As you consider how Laura's experiences may be similar to your own and how your parents' divorce may have affected you throughout your childhood, into adulthood, and still be dogging your life today, bear in mind the following verse in Matthew 11:28, where Jesus says, "Come to me, all you who are weary and burdened, and I will give you rest."

Try the following exercise to help you evaluate if your life pace may be too frantic.

EXERCISE: ORGANIZING YOUR LIFE

Regardless of why your life is frantic, organization can go a long way toward easing the pace. Organizing your life in a healthy way includes sorting through the following elements and putting your life into a comfortable order:

1. What you do;
2. When you do it;
3. For how long;
4. How you feel about it.

Take a piece of paper. Across the top write the headings:

What   *When*   *For How Long*   *Feelings*

Each day for a week, note under the headings what you do, when you do it, for how long, and how you feel about it. This will give you a brief sketch of the present pace you keep in your life.

Now fill out a sketch with the same headings by listing your idea of a "perfect" life pace. Note where there are discrepancies between how you presently live and how you wish you could live.

Think through all the possibilities of how you can make temporary or permanent changes in your pace so that you're doing what suits you best. For instance, if the pace of things at your house has become so frantic that you feel as though you're running a marathon every day, free up time by hiring a part-time gardener, a maid service, or a high school student to run errands for you. Try swapping chores with friends, neighbors, or relatives if you are financially restricted.

Sometimes, our lives get so "crazy" that we fail to notice we are slipping into schedules too structured to allow for any real freedom and we can become slaves to our own organization—we go to the extreme.

A tendency toward extremes is common among adult children of divorce. Often, they have learned to overcompensate in various areas of their lives while trying to meet their basic needs and end up with phobias, addictions, and bad habits.

-3-

The Tendency to Extremes

Along with frantic living, a tendency toward extremes in other areas of life crop up often in the lives of adult children of divorce. Overindulgences with food, money, sex, alcohol, and other drugs seem to be noticeably present in the lives of ACDs. Compulsions, addictions, and obsessions are dangers that ACDs may be well-advised to be sensitive to and watch out for.

On the other end of the spectrum, it is also common for adult children of divorce to take an opposite direction and become especially narrow-minded or judgmental in regard to other people's choices, lifestyles, and ideals. There are many ACDs in religious cults, members of demonstration groups for ultra-conservative causes, and those living in bitter solitude — isolating themselves from mainstream society. Balancing life becomes a vital goal to pursue. What do these tendencies have to do with divorced parents?

Let's look in on a peer support group which is being led by

Russell, an adult child of divorce. His father walked out on him, his mother, and older sister when Russell was only three. Russell's relationship with his father has always been strained.

Russell, now thirty-eight, has undergone years of therapy himself to put his life in order. In the process, Russell's extreme tendency to control his circumstances and the people in his life contributed greatly to the breakdown of his own first marriage. His daughter from this union lives half-way across the country from him most of the year.

Russell's second marriage was crumbling and his other two children were suffering when he finally sought professional help to save himself and the significant relationships in his life.

Russell is a teacher. A few years ago he invited a handful of peers who were also ACDs to get together weekly to discuss their various personal problems. Russell is a natural leader and soon the weekly support group became an extension of his own therapy. Although none of the original attendees still come to the present sessions, there have been four to six others attending on a regular basis since the beginning. As we join them there are four others besides Russell who share their own tendencies to extremes and the emotional problems and personal challenges in their lives that stem from growing up in divorced families.

An ACD Support Group

Kevin, thirty-six, is an engineer and a recovering alcoholic. He is divorced and has three young children, ages two, five, and seven.

Marla, also thirty-six, is a teacher at the same school as Russell. She is a bitter conservative who refuses to believe there is anything good about marriage or family life. She is single and childless.

Dan, thirty-two, is a carpenter and newly obsessed with a religious fervor that seems to alienate most everyone with whom he comes in contact. His wife is frightened and confused by Dan's extremist attitude. The couple doesn't have any children.

Cathy, thirty-four, is a homemaker. She and her husband have one ten-year-old daughter. Cathy is obese and depressed. In the last few years, she and her husband have grown apart.

The five adults meet each Thursday evening in a room at Russell's church where he is an active member, an adult Sunday school teacher and serves on the Board of Education.

Tonight the group begins their discussion with Russell relating a phone encounter he had earlier in the week with his stepfather, Lyle, regarding his mother's medical care.

"I'd like to see what you guys think about something. I called my mother and Lyle Sunday evening, just as I always do. Lyle tells me my mother hasn't been feeling well all week. So, I ask him if he took her to the doctor. Lyle says no, that my mother wouldn't go. But, I tell him, 'You know how she is — she'd have to be practically dead before she'd go on her own — you'll just have to make her go.'

"Well! You'd have thought I put a gun to his head! He starts going on and on about how, yes, he knows my mother and, yes, he knows how to take care of her and he doesn't need *my* advice to be able to handle it!

"I darned near hung up on the old coot! What do you all make of that?" Russell looked at the group expectantly.

They all looked at one another. Who would start? Kevin spoke up first. "To be honest, Russell, it sounds to me like there's been water spilled over that dam before. I can't imagine your stepfather being so intense unless he's felt pressure from you before that he doesn't take good enough care of your mom."

Marla nodded her head, "I agree with Kevin. Have you insinuated that Lyle isn't good enough for your mother in the past?"

"Wait a minute!" Russell snapped. "I never said Lyle wasn't good enough for my mother. All I suggested was that he make her go to the doctor — it's for her own good."

"That's like telling my husband to make me lose weight," Cathy interjected. "Think about it, Russell. Your mother is an adult. If she doesn't take care of herself, that's her choice."

Kevin echoed Cathy's sentiments, "Yeah, Russell, that's

like saying my ex-wife should've been able to force me to stop drinking. That goes against everything we're here for — to learn to understand ourselves better, put our pasts into perspective, and make healthier, more responsible choices for ourselves."

"Okay, okay," Russell held up his arms in surrender, "I see what you mean. I was telling Lyle in so many words that my mother's well-being is his responsibility, not hers, and he wasn't doing a very good job with it."

"Where do you think that comes from?" Dan questioned.

Russell looked at Dan and replied, "I'm not sure. Maybe that my biological father should have taken better care of my mother, and because he didn't, our lives were devastated. Maybe I'm being overprotective again."

"I think that may be," Cathy said. "I remember thinking that every ache, pain, and any other complaint my mother had was my dad's direct fault because he left us to fend for ourselves after the divorce."

Dan said, "I think there are two issues here — as kids we may have resented one or both of our parents for supposedly not taking good care of each other. But I know a lot of ACDs who feel like it was their 'duty' to make sure a stepparent did the taking care of Mom or Dad — and usually the stepparent couldn't do anything quite good enough. And you know, the Lord didn't mean for there to be stepfamilies!"

Kevin ignored the judgmental remark and added, "I think the bottom line here is a feeling of betrayal. I can remember feeling so guilty for enjoying my stepmother more than my real mother. If I'd dared to think consciously that my stepmother took better care of my father than my mom did, then wouldn't that be one more thing to feel guilty about?"

"And isn't it funny," Marla said sarcastically, "that's why we're here at all — we take so many things to the extreme? Who feels neglected, betrayed, used, and abused and for what?"

"Why are you so bitter?" Dan asked Marla.

"Bitter?" Marla looked surprised. "I'm not only bitter, Dan, I'm a realist. I'm not fruity on religion like you!"

Dan's neck immediately turned red. He began to sputter

a retort, but Russell intervened. "Marla, do you think it's fair to ridicule Dan like that?" Russell's leadership abilities smoothly took hold.

Marla lowered her gaze and answered haltingly, "No, I'm sorry, Dan. I know I get carried away sometimes. Your religious beliefs make me very nervous and so they're an easy target for ridicule."

"That was direct and honest, Marla," Russell noted encouragingly. "Dan, do you have anything to say about it?"

"Only to give it to the Lord," Dan said with a televangelistic pride. All four of the others cringed visibly.

Russell changed directions suddenly, "Dan, why do you keep coming to our group sessions?"

Dan was momentarily taken aback before answering, "Why! To be a fisher of men, of course! I am here to be a witness for the Lord and bring hurting souls to His bosom!"

A thick silence hung in the air until Russell spoke, "You know, Dan, I am a Christian and I believe wholeheartedly in living my life as a good and decent person. I know that you are referring to the Bible when you speak of being 'fishers of men.' But have you ever considered that there are many different types of fish in our oceans, lakes, and rivers? Have you stopped to think that all the different kinds are caught with a wide variety of bait?"

"So?" Dan wouldn't make Russell's getting his point across easy.

"So, wouldn't it be worth your time to confront the fact that most fish are caught—regardless of where or with what bait—by quiet persistency? I can't think of one fish I could successfully catch with noisy abrasiveness. I have to give the fish an attractive, positive reason to come to me before there's even an encounter."

Dan seemed irritated. "I don't see what that has to do with me, Russell."

Russell sighed. "Dan, the five of us get together every Thursday night because we have at least two things in common—our parents divorced when we were kids and as adults we each have some tendency toward extremes. Look around. Kevin is a recovering alcoholic, Cathy is overweight, Marla is extremely bitter and conservative, and I have an extreme need to be in control. That brings me back to my first question — why do you come here?"

"Because I have problems left over from when my parents divorced, and I can be an effective witness for the Lord here!" Dan shot right back.

Getting Behind the Reaction to the Problem

Marla sniffed, "Oh, for pete's sake, Dan! Get Russell's point and hear what's being said! You're trying to 'catch fish' by being too extreme and forceful in passing on your religious beliefs! If you ask me, you're hiding behind a public show of religion so you don't have to face your real problems and feelings!"

"Like I hide behind food," Cathy said quietly.

"And I hid behind abusing alcohol," Kevin added.

"I know! I know!" Marla squeezed her mouth into a grimace, "And I hide behind my bitterness!"

Russell smiled, "I think you've just brought the group back to focus, Marla, thank you. I should note my own extreme issue — hiding behind my need to control so that I don't have to face my inner fears and pains. What do you think, Dan? Does what Marla said strike any chords? Do you hide behind your religious beliefs?"

Dan blushed deep red. "I — I — I'm not sure," he stuttered. "I guess I didn't think about 'scaring fish away.' Maybe I am a little extreme in my approach to others. But *not* my beliefs!"

Russell was quick to assure, "Don't get us wrong, Dan. We're not questioning the sincerity of your beliefs. We're saying maybe you're defeating your purpose by how you express your zealous need to 'catch' anything at all and the methods you use to do so."

"Yeah." Marla was not ready to let Dan completely off his own hook yet. "I don't recall Jesus soliciting members to any 'card-carrying Christian club.' If I remember right, He was pretty assertive and true to His example without shoving things down people's throats!"

Kevin rolled his eyes toward heaven and said whimsically, "Father, forgive them, for they do not know what they are doing." Then Kevin looked at Dan intently, "Jesus said that, you know."

"Yes, I know," Dan said, "in Luke 23:34."

Cathy giggled. Russell grinned broadly. Even Dan had to purse his lips to keep from laughing. And Marla sat back in her chair hard and crossed her arms over her chest.

Getting Behind the Problem to the Cause

Russell chose the moment to channel the discussion into a more productive avenue. "I'd like to ask a question. It may seem to have an obvious answer, but I think it's important to discuss. What is the real connection between our parents' divorces and our need to go to one extreme or another to hide from our fears and inner pains? Why do we have this particular Piggy-Back Child?"

Cathy spoke with confidence, "I know my connection. When my parents were divorcing I hated hearing them argue. It made my stomach hurt. I'd overhear them screaming awful things at each other, my stomach would ache, and I'd eat to make the pain go away. As an adult I follow the same behavior. If I have an argument with my husband, a conflict with my daughter, or a confrontation with a neighbor, my stomach hurts and I stuff my face to make it go away!"

Russell nodded with understanding, "And I do a similar thing with the issue of control. When my parents got divorced I felt completely out of control. They bounced me between them like a rubber ball! My dad would say, 'Tell your mother to send more clothes along next time you visit me.' My mom would say, 'Tell your father if he wants you to have more clothes he should buy them!' And on and on. Every time I was with my dad there was something! They played out their power games and resentments through me like an electrical current passes across a wire. I used to sit in my room as a teenager and dream that they would never control me as an adult—then I grew up to need to have control over others!

"Now, when someone says, 'Russell, you should come with us to the beach,' my first thoughts are, 'Only if I can drive, we agree on what we'll do for lunch, and I know what time we'll leave for home.' Spontaneity means out of control to me.

"And I suppose telling Lyle he should make my mother go to the doctor is my way of trying to control Lyle and my mother."

"Hmm," Kevin wondered. "I think maybe that's very parallel to why I started drinking as a teenager. When I couldn't control my parents' behavior I ran away from the pain by getting intoxicated. My parents put me in the middle between them like yours did. I lived with my dad. That made my mom crazy! She took it to be a public statement that she was an unfit parent or something.

"I visited her in the summers and on holidays because my parents lived a thousand miles apart. But when I was with her she made a whole production about how lonely she was because my dad supposedly took me away from her.

"My dad remarried a wonderful woman. And their home really was the better place for a child to grow up. But my mom just couldn't accept the arrangement, so she used me to dump her anger, guilt, and shame into.

"I found out very quickly that getting drunk anesthetized me. As an adult it became natural for me to drink when I had other problems in my life."

Marla put in her two cents. "Well! There's that anger, guilt, and shame thing again! My parents and stepparents were masters at that game! 'Marla, you're too sassy!' 'Marla, you expect too much!' 'Marla, you're too ambitious!' I was too everything and anything for them. My stepfather used to tell me that the only way I'd find a husband who'd put up with me was if I'd shut up and put up like my 'sweet, doting mother.' Of course he would say that! If he told her to spit she'd ask, 'How far?' because, after all, he had to be a good man to take on a woman and three children!

"Of course, his attitude was that he'd put up with her three kids in return for her being his full-time maid and concubine.

"And my stepmother! Brother! She left no doubt from the very beginning about the fact that we were three bratty anchors around her neck! I don't know why my spineless parents never stuck up for themselves or their children!"

Russell asked, "Is it fair to say that you're extremely bitter toward marriage and family life because you feel your home life after your parents' divorce and remarriages was a stream of put-downs and unfair demands? That you felt you could never live up to their standards so you gave up hope?"

"Yes, that's fair," Marla stated. "In fact, it's putting it nicely. I don't want anything to do with a marriage that's going to fall apart anyway and children left to tie me down to a lifetime connection with a man I despise!"

Russell looked at Marla sadly. He wondered silently how the group interaction might help to restore some brightness to Marla's outlook on family life. He knew that anger, guilt, and shame were deeply rooted issues that weren't taken care of in one night. For now, Russell turned to Dan. "How 'bout you, Dan? How do you think your parents' divorce contributes to who you are today?"

Dan looked as though he was thinking really hard for long seconds before answering, "I guess I'd have to say that when my parents got divorced I decided right then and there to win myself back into the Lord's good graces."

Marla began to comment, but Russell interrupted, "How so, Dan?"

"Well, my parents were ostracized from their church after they divorced. I was fourteen when they split up and I know how bad it hurt them to be isolated from the Lord. They gave up trying, but I knew I'd find a way back to His favor some-how."

Russell was instantly filled with compassion and pity for Dan. Here was an adult male, with a fourteen-year-old Piggy-Back Child exposing his pain and fear. This teenager thought his parents' separation from the church meant separation from

God and that it was God who was responsible for the separation. Dan thought he had to earn God's love. The comments
from the group this evening had broken through the false
bravado and pompous attitude about religion behind which
Dan had hidden.

Russell asked him gently, "Do you think we all have to
become 'good enough' before God will bless us, Dan?"

"Well, not really become good enough. You know I'm
'born again' and I know the Lord took me and cleansed me, but
still there's the generational sin of divorce I need to deal with
now."

"And how will you deal with that, Dan?" Russell knew he
would have to take Dan's Piggy-Back Child one small step at a
time in order to help show Dan that God's love was unconditional.

"By being better than them!" Dan spat back. But Russell
knew it wasn't he whom Dan was shouting at—it was his
parents. Dan thought his parents had failed God, and ultimately failed Dan.

"Do you remember what church members said to or about
your parents at the time of their divorce, Dan? Tell me how they
were treated differently after they split."

The Piggy-Back Child Remembers — and Hurts

"I remember all right," Dan asserted. "Before they split up,
my parents were involved in all kinds of church activities
throughout the week. They were invited everywhere! After
Dad moved out of the house, the phone stopped ringing. My
mom cried all the time. I do remember one phone call she got.
After she hung up she had the most awful sadness in her eyes
and she told me the pastor asked her to submit her resignation
from the Board of Music Ministry at the church."

Dan's bottom lip quivered as his fourteen-year-old Piggy-
Back Child watched helplessly as his dear mother agonized
over her alienation from the church she loved. Dan began
hitting his fists against his thighs.

He sobbed out in pain and frustration, "How could a

loving God do that to my gentle mother? She wouldn't hurt anyone!"

Cathy rose from her chair and put an arm across Dan's shoulders, "It'll be all right, Dan," she said softly. "We'll help you work through this."

Even tough-skinned Marla was subdued and looked for-lorn at Dan's breakdown.

Russell thought quickly about what he could do to help Dan. He reached for his Bible and turned to Psalm 34:18 and read aloud, "'The Lord is close to the brokenhearted and saves those who are crushed in spirit.' Dan, God didn't *do* anything to hurt you or your parents! God saves, He doesn't destroy!"

Russell continued quickly before anyone could interrupt the moment, "Dan, it is important to remember that those who alienated and judged your parents were simply human beings acting out of convictions that they apparently felt were right. But they are not God's representatives — they are His children, just like your parents, you, me, or anyone else. God would not turn His back on your parents or tear them down in order to make others feel more worthy of His love! Please believe me, Dan, God loved you and your parents as much the day after they were divorced as He did the day before! The people of the church — mere human beings — had no right to pass judgment on your parents!

"I'm sorry to take so long," Russell looked around the group, "but it's very important to me that you all hear my position on this. God never said that there is only one exact kind of person to be. In fact, 1 Corinthians 12:12–31 talks about all different kinds of 'body parts' and that each part is just as important to the whole as another. There is plenty of room for each one of us to have our own unique relationship with God and to the body. People take verses of the Bible out of context and twist them to mean completely different things than they do within a section of text!

"Dan, your parents are human beings just like everyone else. They make mistakes just like every single one of us. But it doesn't mean God doesn't love them or won't be with them. Dan, I think it would be very helpful for you to get involved in a good Bible study instead of allowing others to frighten you into thinking you have to earn God's approval. If that was the kind of business God was in, there would be no customers from the human race!"

Kevin had been watching Dan closely while Russell was speaking. Dan seemed more collected now. Kevin asked him cautiously, "Do you feel better, Dan?"

Dan looked at Kevin and said gratefully, "Yes, actually I do. I think I've started a great learning journey tonight—a journey to learn about who I am, where I've come from, and where I'm going."

MANAGEMENT: BALANCING EXTREMES

Russell spoke humbly, "Well, I've certainly taken up my share of time talking tonight. Thank you all for your patience! I wonder if we could each address the issue of how we can manage our different extremes and begin to replace the negative reactions our parents' divorces had on us as children with positive, constructive behaviors."

Russell looked to Cathy first. She smiled sheepishly and said, "I guess I need to quit feeding my face with too much food, exercise more, and lose weight."

Kevin smiled affectionately at Cathy, "You know, we could help you to brainstorm ways to stop overeating. I think the key here is learning a healthy balance. You know several self-help groups use a basic, Twelve-Step Program for recovery. I'd like to read a version that's been adapted for the adult children of divorce:

"1. I admitted I was powerless over my parents' divorce and that because of their choice I was deeply affected.
"2. I came to believe that God could restore me to wholeness.
"3. I made a conscious choice to stop blaming my parents for personal problems and turn my will and my life over to the care of God.

"4. I made an honest and genuine appraisal of my personal problems and how they may be related to my parents' divorce.

"5. I admitted to God, to myself, and to another person what my problems were, how they affected those close to me, and that I needed to take responsibility for my behavior.

"6. I confessed to God that I was ready for Him to take away my personal problems and the flaws in my character that may have resulted from growing up in a divorced family.

"7. I asked God sincerely to eliminate the problems and flaws that I was aware of and those I was not aware of.

"8. I made a list of all the suffering that my parents' divorce has caused me and those things that I did in turn that caused suffering for others. I asked God to help me to set things right.

"9. I approached all those people who had suffered due to my behavior and my problems and set things right with them where this was possible without causing them further suffering.

"10. I continue to make honest and genuine appraisals of my personal problems, regardless of where they stem from, and immediately cope with them as awareness dawns.

"11. I spend time daily in prayer, asking God to guide me according to His will and for the strength and courage to follow His direction. I ask Him to give me inner peace about the things in my life that I cannot change.

"12. In appreciation for my own healing and growth, I share the knowledge, wisdom, and understanding that I presently have with others and practice integrity and decency in all my affairs."

Everyone heartily agreed with Kevin that the Twelve-Step Program, adapted for ACDs, was a healthy, loving process to adopt in their own lives.

Dan spoke warmly to Cathy, "I think your overeating is a tremendous pressure on you because the results are visible for the whole world to see. That must be very painful for you."

Cathy's voice quivered with emotion. "Thank you, Dan. That's true. The rest of you can function in the everyday world without exposing your extreme natures if you choose to keep them private. But I can't avoid confronting myself in the mirror every day, knowing that everyone I come in contact with can see my obesity.

"Come on, everyone, what can Cathy do to help herself to stop overeating?" Kevin asked optimistically.

Marla spoke, "The first thing I'd do is join an additional support group, one specifically for battling weight problems."

"Good point, Marla!" Russell declared. "Support groups and professional counseling for stubborn problems are two of the best ways to help put or keep our lives in balance. In my opinion, these are the safest ways to prevent ourselves from being overwhelmed by issues that keep us overreacting in extreme ways."

"I agree," said Kevin, "I doubt I could stay sober more than a few months without surrounding myself with loving, supportive peer groups. I went to individual counseling for several weeks when I was newly sober. Now I go to Alcoholics Anonymous meetings weekly. There's a big difference between forcing yourself not to eat to lose weight and gently changing the life patterns that cause you to overdo in the first place. The difference is—quality of life."

"I agree," Marla joined in, "the quality of our lives is the clincher. Look at me—single, alone, and bitter. What kind of quality protection does this provide for my life?"

This was the first time in several weeks that Russell had heard Marla admit any real possibility that she might be completely miserable in her chosen lifestyle.

Russell asked Marla, "What else do you think Cathy could do to stop overeating besides group support or individual counseling work?"

"Hmm," Marla put a thumb under her chin and thought.

"I think when she has conflict and her stomach starts to ache she could replace eating with something else—exercising, writing in a diary, or gardening. Therapeutic stuff like that could help her break her habit."

"Excellent idea!" Russell commended. "I think we should all take home what you just said to use for our different extreme reactions. Has anything similar worked for you in staying sober, Kevin?"

"As a matter of fact, it has," Kevin acknowledged. "Especially in the beginning, when I would crave a drink so badly my whole body hurt, I would try to replace the inner calling to drink with a new, healthy reaction. For example, I would take a walk, call a friend, or read on the patio. Changing locations of where I usually give in to a compulsive behavior helps to break the chain of events that set me up to bring me down!"

Russell turned to Dan, "What do you think Cathy could do to help her overeating?"

Dan cleared his throat. He was still a little uncomfortable from his traumatic self-discovery earlier. Tentatively, he said, "I guess my first thoughts are: to pray for help, keep only good foods around that can be eaten in place of bad ones—carrots instead of candy—and observe how happy, thin people live."

"Great points, Dan!" Russell affirmed. "I think observing people who live balanced, healthy lives is another point for all of us to take to heart. I don't mean putting people on pedestals or making them our idols, but learning by example is a powerful way to change!"

"I guess so!" Marla said sarcastically. "We're all here in the first place because we learned things so well from the rotten examples our parents set!"

Russell looked at Marla directly, "I don't think it's fair to say our parents set completely rotten examples. They did the best they could with what they had to work with at the time. I don't believe for a minute that parents try to hurt or overburden their children on purpose. It's vital that we remember as adults that who we are today is influenced by how we reacted to and perceived our circumstances as children. We need to help our

Piggy-Back Children to grow up to integrate with what we know and understand as adults."

"By all means!" Kevin added. "Our parents didn't get married planning to get divorced and pull their families apart. They're people just like us. Our tendencies to extremes come more from the carry-over reactions of Piggy-Back Children than logical adult ones."

Cathy had sat silent for a long while. Now she contributed, "I think an essential ingredient to balancing our lives is to forgive our parents for the chaos their choices brought into our worlds when we were children. I think I need to stop blaming my parents for the ache in my stomach, realize that the physical reaction is coming from the little Piggy-Back Child, and help her to see it's not necessary to kick me in the stomach every time there's tension now."

Russell watched as all heads nodded. He asked plainly, "What are things we can do to help our hurting, Piggy-Back Children to grow up, and through this process help eliminate our tendency toward extremes?"

Kevin answered, "I think Cathy's point is an excellent one. We may not be able to forgive our parents for everything they did to hurt us, but we can begin by trying to forgive them for their choice to divorce in the first place.

"Beyond that, I've found that it's essential for me to love myself—both as an adult with problems and as a hurting, confused Piggy-Back Child. When I truly love myself then I stop beating myself up for all the negative things I've done and weaknesses I have. I see clearly now that I was not responsible for my parents' choice to divorce or how they chose to behave afterward. As a sober individual, I realize that there was no genuine blame to put on my parents for my choice to drink. Nobody can make me do anything. I must live with the fact that I chose to drink in reaction to painful circumstances. And that's what I, as an adult, say to myself as a frightened child. I am growing my Piggy-Back Child up by teaching myself that I have choices. As an adult I choose more appropriate and healthier ways to cope with pain and heartache."

"Valuable information, Kevin!" Russell said appreciatively. "I'd like to review the points that have been made in regard to balancing and managing our lives better:

"1. Adopt a Twelve-Step Program philosophy as a permanent lifestyle.

"2. Join peer support groups or go to individual counseling.

"3. Begin to replace extremist habits with constructive reactions to pain. For example, take a walk instead of eating, drinking, imposing your beliefs, trying to control others, or isolating yourself in bitterness.

"4. Physically change your surroundings when you're severely tempted to give in to a negative reaction — go to a friend's, shopping, or even just another room.

"5. Pray for help and strength to risk changing lifelong patterns that are destructive to your well-being.

"6. Replace a healthy object for an unhealthy one. For instance, carrots for candy, mineral water for alcohol, etc.

"7. Observe how well-adjusted people balance their lives with fair amounts of work, play, rest, and contemplation.

"8. Begin to integrate your Piggy-Back Child with your adult self by forgiving your parents for the pain that their choice to divorce caused you.

"9. Stop blaming your parents for your destructive habits — realize that you're reacting negatively from your Piggy-Back Child's perspective, not your mature adult's.

"10. Try to work on truly loving yourself by being kind to and accepting of the person you are.

"11. Realize that as a child you had no choice in your parents' divorce or how they behaved afterward — but you do have a choice now in how you behave!"

Russell finished with a smile. Even Marla appeared to be content. Kevin brought up something that had occurred to him earlier.

"It seems like Cathy's overeating became the reference point from which we worked tonight and I want you to know I appreciate you for cooperating with that, Cathy! We could've chosen any one of our problems to dissect and brainstorm about. I hope you know we weren't picking on yours!"

Cathy's cheeks turned a warm pink, "Thanks, Kevin. It makes me feel good that you considered my reaction! I do understand and don't feel picked on at all!"

Russell thought they'd certainly covered a lot of ground this evening and brought out many important feelings and helps to work with regarding their tendencies to extremes. He closed the group session by asking each person to think of a goal to work toward balancing their behavior that they could share with the group the next week.

EXERCISE: EVENING UP THE SCALES

If you have a tendency to extremes, chances are your life scales are "weighted" to one side in one or several areas of your life. We'll look at evening up the scales for one example, below, but the same steps apply to any tendency to extreme:

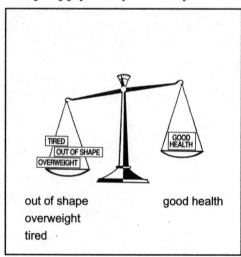

Figure 1

Balancing Steps:

1. Take a good, hard look at yourself as you really are.
2. Gauge how badly or how well you feel about yourself.
3. List the things you'd like to change about yourself.
4. List specific things you can do to make the changes.
5. Break the list of things you can do into palatable chunks of attainable goals.
6. Do one chunk at a time, until each one has been worked through so that you have balanced "scales."

Trish is a forty-year-old ACD. She, just as Cathy and millions of others, has battled to lose an extra twenty pounds nearly all her adult life. She tends to go on fad diets, lose up to ten pounds, get frustrated, and finally give up. She's made up her mind this time to get rid of her Piggy-Back Child once and for all!

It's important to remember, however, that a Piggy-Back Child usually frightens easily, leans toward stubbornness, and will fight like mad to hang on. Just as it does no lasting good to slap a child around, it will do no permanent good to abuse a Piggy-Back Child either. She must be guided in how to get off your back and loved into your adult personality.

Even when the Piggy-Back Child gets down you may have to let her walk with you hand-in-hand for awhile until she can comfortably diffuse herself into your wholeness.

For example, Trish would take a good, hard look at herself and know she needed to lose weight to get healthier. She easily gauged that she felt badly enough about her appearance that she wanted to lose twenty pounds. She listed diets and exercise plans she could follow to get in shape many times.

In this way, Trish's Piggy-Back Child was identified and coaxed to attention. Then Trish would jump headlong into a crash program to lose weight. She'd take off around ten pounds — the Piggy-Back Child was listening and even had the courage to hop to the ground!

But instead of breaking her goals into palatable chunks that she could deal with, Trish tried to push and force herself with unrealistic nutritional sacrifices and amounts of exercise. She didn't follow through with her plans lovingly. In other words, she tried to escape her Piggy-Back Child too quickly and the Piggy-Back Child bolted right back up around Trish's neck! Now instead of walking with the Piggy-Back Child gently to success, Trish was in greater pain and deeper failure than before—each time she tried to lose her twenty pounds it took longer to get started and more effort to lose even ten pounds. The Piggy-Back Child wasn't so easily comforted in the repeated attempts.

Only when Trish got on a safe diet and a slowly increasingly difficult exercise plan from her medical doctor, and then followed through on it safely, did the Piggy-Back Child of overweight finally release Trish to achieve her goal.

Sometimes the roots of reacting to various life circumstances come from the Piggy-Back Child's basic insecurity about himself and the instability of life. When a couple gets married, they usually intend for their union to be forever. When a divorce happens, it quite often shakes those involved to the very core and their perception of stability and security becomes what lasts forever!

We will explore the problems of insecurity in the next chapter and discover how they may be managed.

-4-

Insecurity:
A Growing Problem

The emotional battering and bruising caused by disappointments, traumas, and upheavals that normally surround divorce spills over into the lives of the children with incredible impact. Divorce isn't something that goes on for a few months and then passes gently into the nostalgic past!

Children of divorce commonly grow up with deep-seated insecurities about who they are, what strings may be attached to relationships, when their lives might fall apart—again—under their very noses, and how their real or imagined flaws could be "discovered" and then, in turn, rejected.

As youngsters, "forever" became a short while for children of divorce. The insecurities that haunt them can be devastating to their mental, physical, emotional, and spiritual health.

A Child's Perception

Jack's parents divorced when he was twelve. He clearly remembers the evening his dad left home. "I got home from school and my parents were sitting at the dining room table. I could tell Mom had been crying and Dad just looked tired. When my teenaged brother and sister got home awhile later, my parents called us to sit at the table with them.

"My dad told us that he and my mom had decided that it would be better for everyone in the family if he moved out of the house.

"Before he could even go on my sister, who was in ninth grade, spouted, 'Great! Just great! Now I suppose you're going to get divorced and embarrass us all!' The rest of us just stared at her."

Jack recalls that after several seconds his dad resumed speaking. Between them his parents explained that they just didn't get along any more and needed to separate for some time to think things through.

Jack remembers his sixteen-year-old brother as being completely stoic and not responding at the moment with any emotion.

"Later, though," Jack relates, "I found him crying in the bathroom. But he got angry at me for walking in and told me to leave him alone. My sister locked herself in her room and turned up her music real loud. I just sort of floated from room to room seeing what everyone else was doing. Mom was cooking dinner like usual and Dad was packing suitcases like he was leaving for a business trip.

"I can remember wondering, *What is wrong with all of you?! Our family is falling apart here and you're just going about your business!* I'm sure each of us was going through our own emotional reaction to the upset, but it seemed to me that we were turning our backs on one another, letting the family slip away. I think I decided that afternoon that I couldn't ever really depend on anyone—at some point people would always let me down."

Jack looks very sad as he remembers himself as a lonely, confused little boy wandering throughout his house that day.

"We actually sat up to the table for dinner like nothing was wrong! We ate almost in silence. Nobody asked any of the hundreds of questions that must have been running through our minds. My parents didn't offer us one bit of additional information. When we finished eating they went to their room and we kids cleaned up. We could hear Mom and Dad talking. Sometimes one of them would raise their voice, then the other would, then their conversation would become low and muffled. When we were done cleaning up, the three of us went to the den and stared at the television.

"After what seemed like hours my dad came in and simply said, 'I'm leaving now. Come give me a hug good-bye.' We dutifully sent our dad packing without a tear. As he shut the door, he did have the decency to tell us he'd see us soon. That was it—my dad was gone. From my perspective my family as I'd known it since birth was over in the space of a few hours."

Jack spent the next several years living with a mother who picked herself up, dusted herself off, and began dating. Jack never did keep track of all the male friends who filed through their lives. There was the musician, the executive, the mechanic, the traveling salesman, the English teacher, the plumber, and on and on. Jack labeled them all according to their profession.

Even now, Jack's mother seems to have a different beau at every family get-together. Jack's own children are teenagers and have grown accustomed to their worldly grandma. But Jack still has a hard time with his relationship with her.

"I can remember visiting my dad in his tiny, two-room apartment. I felt so sorry for him. He seemed like a lost kitten in the middle of all his dirty dishes, laundry, and newspapers. Trying to fit all three of us kids in the apartment was a joke, so he started picking us up at the house and we'd go somewhere that was supposed to be fun—the zoo, science center, historical museum, amusement park, and every other 'attraction' within an hour from home. After a few months his girlfriend, Sally, started joining our outings. My dad began to smile a lot. Pretty soon, my sister refused to go see Dad on the weekends and my brother just sat around looking sullen.

"Next thing I knew Dad was telling us how he loved Sally and he hoped we would be happy for him because he and Sally were getting married. Sure enough, we were in the front pew of a church several weeks later, watching our dad promise to love and cherish *Sally*—forever."

Jack opens his palms and shrugs his shoulders, "What can a guy say? I celebrated my fourteenth birthday at Dad and Sally's house. There was a big fight between my parents over where I'd be on my special day. Dad won because it was his Saturday to have me. Sally was real nice. She had cake and ice cream, party hats, balloons, and the whole deal. They bought me lots of presents. Somewhere in between the divorce and his marriage to Sally my dad must have gotten a raise or something because he and Sally lived a pretty decent lifestyle materially— until about five years later when *they* got divorced.

"I wasn't quite nineteen when Dad told me that Sally was leaving him for another man. At least they didn't have children together! My dad sold their big, nice house and bought a small, modest home in a less exclusive part of town. I remember overhearing my mom tell a friend. 'It serves him right, I knew that little twit would take him for everything she could get! Thank heaven she couldn't get to my house or the kids' college funds'!"

Jack looks contemplative, "That's how my life went from age twelve until I married Linda after college graduation—bits and pieces of memories floating down a stream. Nothing important was ever really stable. Up and down emotionally. One day my dad was in a dinky apartment, the next a big house, and the next a small cottage. One day a piano was delivered to my house because Mom was dating the musician, and the next a truck came and got it because they broke up. One day Mom was wearing turquoise and cowboy boots because she was dating a ranch dude and the next she was buying fake diamonds to go to a dinner with the corporate lawyer. Bits and pieces. To this day there are questions I have never asked."

Questions from the Piggy-Back Child

Jack looks off into space as he ticks off some of the questions he's grown up with in his mind:

Why couldn't my parents get along?
Was it because of us kids?
Weren't we good enough?
Did they love us the same as before their divorce?
Who decided who got the kids?
Did one want us more than the other?
Did they wish we'd never been born?
Is there something I could've done to save their marriage?
Did they ever wish they'd stayed together?
What would I be like if they had?
Would we be poor or rich?
Would my sister still have gotten into drugs?
Would my brother still be trapped in a rotten marriage?
Would we have hated one another?
Why did my mother date so many men?
Why did my dad marry and divorce a second time?
How do people know they don't love each other any more?
Could they just be going through a phase?
Couldn't they fall in love again?
How could they forget why they got married at all?

Often, there are so many questions surrounding parents' divorces that they are woven into the fabric of the children's personalities. They wind up contributing to the deep insecurities that so many ACDs have as adults. The Piggy-Back Child of insecurity haunts adult children of divorce by whispering constant questions, doubts, and skeptical notes into their ears that shake them up.

There was such emotional distance in Jack's family that he couldn't bring himself to approach his parents for answers to his questions. Instead, he discusses possible answers with his wife of nearly twenty years. Linda knows Jack's insecurities well. She has been a loving support for him and understands that it's still hard for him to believe that she loves him unconditionally and won't just up and leave him some day on a whim—or because she discovers something "awful" about him that causes her to stop loving him.

Conditional Love

Linda is from a functional, nuclear family. She has gotten upset with Jack's parents many times over the course of her marriage as she has helped Jack work through problems that stem from his childhood experiences following their divorce.

Linda says, "I wish more parents would realize how their divorces and the putting back together of their lives affects their children. There are parts of Jack's personality that are still fragmented as the result of his various insecurities. Sometimes we must take apart, piece by piece, an irrational reaction he has to some incident, analyze it, and put his sense of proportion back together again.

"For example, our teenage daughter is going steady with a very nice boy. When she showed us a lovely ring he got her for her birthday, Jack nearly went off the deep end! He fussed and fumed about how terrible this was and that she had to give the ring back to her boyfriend. Finally, I said, 'Enough is enough! It's just a gift, Jack. What is the bottom line here?!'

"After hours of discussion and rooting around in his past, Jack realized that even the thought of his daughter caring enough about someone to have a committed relationship scared the stuffing out him. To him, that ring said commitment and commitments in Jack's eyes will eventually be broken—he is frightened to his very insides that his kids will get dumped on one day by broken promises, as he was.

"We had to talk and talk about taking normal risks in relationships and not being able to protect our kids from their own choices or those of others. There just aren't any guarantees in life."

Linda shakes her head, "You know, divorcing parents could help their children feel so much more secure if they would talk to the kids! Tell them what's going on in vocabulary their children can relate with. Here Jack and I have been married for almost two decades and there are still isolated incidents when he's afraid that our lives will just fall apart one afternoon — as if he'll come home from work on a Tuesday and I'll banish him to the two-room apartment he remembers his father living in. That's insecurity!

"Jack's healing and growth has been a long process of renewal. Most of the time he's okay, but there are still those times of reaction that are from his subconscious, when his Piggy-Back Child tells Jack that things are going too well — something's gotta give — and Jack panics. Then he has to take each situation, one at a time, and overcome his problems piece by piece.

"I understand that life happens, and divorce happens, and things can get out of our control. But for the adult children of divorce I know, including Jack, it can be excruciatingly painful to wonder if your whole world will quake some morning and force you to shift your entire life position for reasons you can't understand.

"From my perspective, Jack's most dominant question since the day his parents split up has been, 'Am I so unlovable that from here on out people will leave me?' Think about how it looks and feels to a kid to go to school or soccer practice one day and come home to find his mom's or dad's bags packed!

"Jack remembers going over in his mind again and again the day his parents split to see if there was something one of the kids did the night before that may have caused the breakup. We adults forget that kids just don't process things the same way we do.

"You know what it was like the first time you went back to a childhood place you remembered as being huge, and when you saw it as an adult it looked almost miniature? That's how distorted things can get for the adult children of divorce."

Even When Kids Know It's Not Their Fault

Even the ACDs who shared their stories, and who knew from the start that their parents' divorces were not their fault, felt similar insecurities left over from childhood. This also included the ACDs who were relieved that their parents split because of domestic violence, blatant adultery, complications of alcohol, or other drug abuse, etc.

Regardless of the circumstances surrounding divorce, there are common, underlying issues of insecurity that many adult children of divorce must resolve—questions that must be reconciled with healthy answers:

1. Am I lovable—flaws and all?
2. Will my life fall apart unexpectedly?
3. Will the people I love reject me?

And there is an immense insecurity that can lurk in the shadows of the minds of ACDs as the all-time question of questions—the Grand-Daddy Fear:

"If my parents didn't love me enough to stay together (remember the distortions of childhood minds) *then how much worse will it be if God deserts me or 'gets' me?"*

If God allows little children to go through such traumas as divorce—*what* might He allow to happen to those children when they're grown up and make mistakes of their own? Horror of horrors! God becomes someone either to be feared to the depths of a soul or rejected completely—largely because of unspoken anxieties, unasked questions, misunderstood circumstances, misinterpretation of people's behavior, and distorted images of events long past.

However, adult children of divorce also fear or reject God because they think He hasn't helped them through the pain of their circumstances. They believe God didn't protect them or their parents from the suffering of splitting their families apart. In their eyes God let them down.

Little children aren't as afraid to question God. They often know instinctively that He has wide shoulders and they can ask Him about or challenge Him with anything. But adults usually are more inhibited about poking around God with too many questions—other than "Why??!!" when things don't go our way. Adults may be leery of bringing something to God's attention, just as you might feel in voluntarily stopping a patrolman to let him know your car license is expired. Generally, we don't like to stir up any trouble for ourselves.

Consequently, we may harbor destructive questions and negative feelings (toward ourselves, others, and God) for long periods of time. Like acid, these can eat away at our insides until we become mere shells of the people God provided for us to become.

Ironically, God waits patiently for us to question Him, to challenge Him, to interact with Him, and to have a full relationship with Him. When Job questioned God, God didn't strike the man dead—He answered Job, usually with more questions!

If a little one stood outside your patio door with her nose pressed to the glass, would you ignore her and go about your life as if she weren't there? Or would you ask her what she wanted or needed from you? If you thought she had destroyed your family life, then had the nerve to stand at your patio door, wouldn't you be even more eager to get things settled with her?

God is no different. He waits at the doors of our hearts. He allows us to go about our business in the hope that we'll notice Him, talk with Him, have the decency to give Him a chance to explain that He didn't destroy our lives, and in the hope that we'll allow Him to stay in our lives permanently.

In Revelation 3:20, Jesus says, "Here I am! I stand at the door and knock. If anyone hears my voice and opens the door, I will come in and eat with him, and he with me."

For many adult children of divorce a great insecurity about the answers to deep life questions are illusive and very threatening. But there is One who stands with His face pressed against the door to the heart.

Jack's wife, Linda, describes it this way, "Jack has told me that as a young adult he viewed God as a giant who stood eye level with the top of a fruit tree and rattled the branches. The fruit that couldn't hang on and fell to the ground, God stepped on and squashed. In Jack's mind, he lived with the insecurity that God could decide at any given moment, on any given day, to shake him out of the tree and stomp on him!

"You can see the same old pattern of insecurities:

"1. Am I lovable enough — flaws and all — for God?

"2. Will God wreak havoc on my life at any second?

"3. Will God reject me?

"Talk about the ultimate insecurity! To an adult child of divorce, the very fabric of life becomes insecure if God can't be depended upon. It's taken Jack a long time to learn to trust God. There have been many tears and much despair as he struggled to allow himself to put his faith in God. Jack eventually accepted that he just wasn't going to wake up one morning and know all the answers to all his questions or have his life be magically all right. He became more willing to let each day roll along and see what happened."

MANAGEMENT: DEVELOPING SELF-CONFIDENCE

To reduce, and hopefully eliminate, the insecurities that can haunt adult children of divorce, it is essential to develop self-confidence.

Self-confidence means to have trust and assurance in one's own abilities and judgment.

Insecurity, on the other hand, is to feel unsafe or beset by anxieties. To eliminate unnecessary anxieties, it is vital to learn to trust in one's own abilities to carry on the business of life.

In Jack's case, his first step toward this was to ask the many questions he had about life and God. He asked his wife, Linda, he asked himself, and he asked God.

If you are an ACD and your parents are still living, it may be very helpful to sit down with them, call or write them, and ask them questions that have bothered you. If your parents and/or stepparents are open and will answer your questions, write down their answers so that you can look back on them later and piece together a mental profile of what life was like from their perspective during and following the divorce. As an adult, the answers to these questions may help you see your growing up in the aftermath of divorce from a completely different perspective. You may begin to realize that many of your insecurities arise from childish distortions of the way you thought things were, fears of how they might have become, or fantasies about how you wish things could have been.

If your parents are no longer living, or emotional tensions prevent your actually asking them your questions, write them down anyway. Ask a spouse, peer, counselor, or other trusted adult to help you consider what the answers to your questions might be as you look at them as an adult yourself.

With Linda's help, Jack began to realize that he did not have to be tied irrevocably to the pain from his childhood. He needed to learn to believe that he was absolutely and unconditionally entitled to love, acceptance, inner peace, help, joy, and forgiveness — that he was a child of God.

Linda grew up in a home where her feelings of self-worth were nurtured. She was self-confident and secure. She entered adulthood feeling very much a part of God's family and never doubted that the privileges of membership were rightfully hers.

Jack, however, couldn't see the simplicity of this concept. His image of parents was anything but secure and confident. God, as a perfect Father, seemed too much fantasy instead of reality.

Linda explained to Jack, "Look, you responded to what you saw from your parents, but the Bible tells us in 2 Corinthians 5:7, 'We live by faith, not by sight.' And in verse 17 it says, 'Therefore, if anyone is in Christ, he is a new creation; the old has gone, the new has come!' You can let go of the scars you carry from your past. You can forgive your parents for being human just like you and me. Then you can choose to put your faith in something you can't see with your eyes or feel with your hands but is bigger than all of us!"

In the beginning it was extremely difficult for Jack to make even a tiny dent in letting go of his insecurities or to put the smallest amount of trust in God. In fact, he thought Linda was a little kooky with her Bible quoting. He knew what happened when those "Bible-beating Christians" got going—they steamrolled right over people!

Fortunately, Linda was a Christian who lived an inoffensive example of her beliefs. As Jack watched her go exuberantly through life, he began to appreciate her self-confidence and the security she exuded. Even though he was still insecure and doubting, changes were beginning deep inside him of which he wasn't even conscious.

Jack was so insecure in the first years of their marriage that if Linda was fifteen or twenty minutes late getting home from work he'd be in an uproar thinking she had been in an accident or was having an affair.

One evening as Linda turned her key in the lock she heard Jack pacing back and forth across the kitchen floor. She glanced at her watch. She was half an hour late. Even before she saw Jack's face, Linda knew how agitated he was. Sure enough, he lit into her about his being worried sick, stalking around, and wondering what to do—call the hospitals, the police or what?

Linda, who had been held up at work by an unpleasant encounter with a dissatisfied client, was not about to listen to any more criticisms today. She looked Jack in the eye and said with quiet restraint, "Jack, stop doubting and believe in me! Please let me help you get a handle on this! You'll never feel at peace if you don't stop being afraid to live and let me live too!"

Jack was taken aback by Linda's reaction and stood in silence for several seconds before he replied, "I'm sorry, Linda, I really am sorry."

Linda went to Jack, put her arms around him and held him close. Lovingly she said, "Jack, I can't give you any guarantees that the future will be completely free from tragedy—we have to live one day at a time and accept that each of us is an important link in the chain of life. If you are afraid to live, then life becomes death."

Jack hugged Linda back tightly and whispered, "That's my

whole problem in a nutshell—I'm so insecure that I'm afraid to live."

Linda's eyes glistened with tears, "Jack, I love you very much, but I can't continue to live like this. I can't go on walking on eggshells with you."

"Okay, Linda, okay," Jack said with quiet resolve. "I'll try it your way."

"It's not my way, Jack. It's not something you take from me. It's something you choose as your way."

"It's just so hard," Jack moaned. "I look at you, the kids, and our lives, and if I lost what we have I just couldn't take it!"

"Jack, if you lost every single thing tomorrow, you *could* take it. You are more than the product of the people and things in your life. Yes, it would be a terrible thing to have to deal with—the most crushing situation life could probably hand out to you—but you would survive! Life here is temporary and passing away every day from birth until death. In between those two, once we are old enough to make decisions for ourselves, we must choose to live!"

Jack's eyes twinkled as he looked at his lovely wife, "All right! I choose to live!"

What's the Worst That Could Happen?

After Jack consciously chose to cope with his insecurity he began to see many things about his life in a newer and healthier way.

He adopted a "What's-the-worst-that-could-happen?" attitude for every area of his life. If he found himself in a jam at work and was threatened by anxiety, he asked himself, "What's the worst that could happen?"

In the beginning, the answers scared him almost as much as the situation. He could be fired if he didn't perform well at work. Linda could die of a heart attack if she didn't take care of herself. The kids could be paralyzed if he let them go out for dangerous sports. Linda could divorce him if he didn't resolve his insecurity.

Gradually, Jack could feel the answers frightening him less because he was bringing them into his conscious thoughts and choosing to go ahead and live in spite of his fears. Little by little the dark, murky shadows of insecurity gave way to light, uplifting hope. Jack found he had more energy for constructive things. Eventually, when he had an insecure thought, he would get control by simply telling himself over and over, "Do not fear. Do not fear." And one day he realized he hadn't had any anxious moments for many weeks in a row.

When surprise "attacks" hit him, as when his teenage daughter received the ring from her boyfriend, Jack and Linda put into motion a pact they'd made — no matter how small the issue, they would hash it over until the root of the problem was found and a way to accept or resolve it was dug out.

Jack found himself able to appreciate life more and more. On a warm Saturday afternoon while he was in the garden, it occurred to him that he had not been plagued for many months by the incessant questions and anxieties which had haunted him before.

He began keeping in touch more often with his parents. His conversations were much more pleasurable and less tense. He knew that he had really, truly accepted them as people, and that he loved them for who they were, not for who he wished they were. That happened when he could comfortably invite his mother and her boyfriend-of-the-moment for a surprise birthday party he gave for Linda.

Of course, ACDs are not the only ones who have problems with insecurities. But they have a delicate and special sensitivity to the changing tides of life. Given successful attempts to develop self-confidence, adult children of divorce can become free to enjoy life to the full each day because healthy ACDs know and appreciate deep within them the truth of Jesus' instructions in Matthew 7:34, "Therefore do not worry about tomorrow, for tomorrow will worry about itself. Each day has enough trouble of its own."

ACDs have a certain knowledge and understanding of the fact that nothing in this world is guaranteed to last forever. Each day holds the possibility of tragedy, chaos, heartbreak, and trauma. Healthy ACDs also know that each day can bring new joys, successes, insights, and loves.

If we allow ourselves to dwell on the dark possibilities of life, then we deliberately choose insecurity for our lives. But if we choose to allow the light of optimism and hope to shine in our lives we choose to move toward self–confidence. Note that regardless of our fears and insecurities, *we do make the choice!* We will be accountable to our choices in life no matter which way we go!

Jack offers an outline of the steps he has taken in moving forward, away from his insecurities, toward self-confidence:

1. Make a list of all the questions you can think of that you have mulled around in your mind since your parents divorced.
2. Ask your parents these questions in person, by phone, or in a letter. If you can't do this, try to think through what the answers may be with someone you trust.
3. Consciously choose to believe that you are absolutely, unconditionally entitled to love, acceptance, inner peace, help, joy, and forgiveness in your life — that you are a child of God.
4. Accept by faith that God is *not* like your earthly parents — He is God. We don't need to know all the answers to our questions; we can trust that things will be all right.
5. Consciously choose to believe that you can forgive your parents for being human, even if you can't forgive them for some specific hurts they've caused you at this point in your life.
6. Try to stop doubting that you can live a joyful, fulfilling life.
7. Reach out to someone for help — your spouse, friend, counselor, or pastor.
8. Make a choice to live — in spite of your insecurities.

9. Adopt a "What's-the-worst-that-could-happen?" policy for your life.
10. Confront your fears by living right through them to help desensitize yourself to insecurities.
11. Resolve to dig in and figure out ways to solve those "surprise" attacks of insecurity.
12. Resolve that you will live each new day as it comes and not fret and fuss about what trouble tomorrow may bring.

Insecurity is a tough problem to deal with. To develop self-confidence it's important to try new things, add some variety and new goals to your life. Trying new things allows you to experience that whether you succeed, fail, or are indifferent to something doesn't matter so much as the doing of them does — taking control of your activities and developing a sound self-image. Going through the motions helps you to gain momentum and eventual control over your insecurity. Try the following exercise to see how experimenting with new things may help you become more secure.

EXERCISE: TRYING NEW THINGS

1. Pick a sport, hobby, place, or job you've always dreamed of getting involved in or simply feel curious about.

2. Get more familiar with your "new thing"; read related books and articles; attend related events as a spectator at games, exhibitions, conventions, or trade shows; go to adult education classes; gradually work up to some level of participation. For example, if you want to try a new career idea, get a part-time job, or an apprenticeship in a specific position, try it on awhile.

3. If you start into something new and find you don't like it or that it's too difficult to devote your time and energy to right now, leave this thing and go on to another. If you don't like it, you've succeeded at finding that out. If it's too demanding for now, but you seem to love it, you can save this thing for later.

With each new thing you try and succeed at, you increase your self-confidence. This self-assurance helps to eliminate insecurities by exercising your power of choice and offering the experiences of saying yes, no, or maybe at your discretion in nonthreatening circumstances.

Then, when you come up against a tough decision that you'd ordinarily quake at making, or maybe go along with the crowd so as not to cause any waves, you'll have more confidence in your own judgment.

If your insecurities are manifested in jealousy and possessiveness, you may find after practicing new things that your self-image begins to grow and, as you feel more adequate within yourself, your feelings of threat may disappear.

If you're too insecure to try new things that are "big," try them in a "miniature" version. For example, if you want to try farming, start with an herb, flower, or vegetable garden. If you want to hunt big game in Africa, read about native animals, visit zoos, and hunt smaller prey closer to home first. If you've always wanted to go on a cruise, but are afraid, stay a few days on a rented houseboat before you spend the money to set sail on the sea.

It's Not Selfish to Assert

If you are too insecure to be assertive, sit down with a pencil and paper. Write down typical situations where you usually want to say no but can't seem to get enough nerve to do so. For example:

1. When asked to be on committees;
2. When asked to baby-sit a friend's children;
3. When expected to host big family get-togethers.

Now write down a repertoire of responses that are clear "no's" without being rude or tacky:

1. "Thank you for asking, but my time is already committed to other things."
2. "I'm sorry, I have to say no this time."
3. "It won't work out for me then."
4. "I can't, because my schedule is already full."

Whatever responses you prefer, practice them aloud, watch yourself in the mirror until your body language reflects confident posture and your voice is strong and clear.

Try your new responses as often as you get the opportunity until you're strong enough to pick and choose between what you will or will not accept as responsibilities.

Arising from a deep fear of change, ACDs commonly try to provide security for themselves by exercising a great need for consistency. This need is intertwined with insecurity and can get quite out of hand if left unchecked.

A life that is structured so as to try to avoid change is destined for tremendous downfalls and is stifling at best — even life-threatening in some cases.

For individuals who were traumatized by their parents' divorces when they were small children or young adults, there can be a lingering need to keep the status quo in their lives — no matter what the price. Like the small child who spins himself dizzy and then gropes to find something rigid to steady himself, an adult child of divorce often "clears his head" by settling into rigid routines fairly early in life.

In the next chapter we will see how devastating and defeating too much consistency can be for those who refuse to risk important life changes.

-5-

The Great Need for Consistency

Do you ever get irritated by people who refuse, for no apparent reason, to change things in their lives? Maybe a wife won't change her hairstyle or try a new clothing style because she likes her "old way." Possibly a man must keep a hairbrush or alarm clock in precisely the same spot or it unsettles him. Some people drive older model cars or keep outdated furniture long after they have served their purpose. Some men get rattled if the remote control to the television has been moved or the evening newspaper isn't by their favorite chair each night after dinner.

There are all kinds of harmless idiosyncrasies that we have in our personal lives. One family network is upset if dinner isn't on the table by 6:00 P.M. Another must clean the whole house every Saturday morning without fail. Sometimes we have consistent patterns because they make us feel safe or just because they are mindless habits.

91

But sometimes we won't change something in our lives because we're scared witless of what might happen if we do. Sometimes we make conscious choices not to change; the thought of finding new employment, even if we hate our present jobs, may be too frightening. At other times, our subconscious tells us not to change; if we don't visit our parents regularly may be they'll stop loving us.

For the adult children of divorce, consistency can be a driving need and a particularly difficult issue to confront. Many ACDs refuse to get divorced, not because of personal reasons or moral values, but *only* because their parents did, and they won't, period.

There are ACDs who balk at disrupting their lives with major changes such as moving, finding new jobs, getting married, or having a baby. These things are too near the core of their most chaotic life change—their parents' divorce.

It is difficult enough for many ACDs to change the recipes they like, the tennis rackets they use, or the water holes they fish, much less initiate big changes voluntarily.

The need for consistency can be so great it puts a stranglehold not only on the individual ACD but also on his spouse, children, and other loved ones. Those who care about an adult child of divorce must often stand aside and watch helplessly as the ACD refuses to partake willingly of healthy change.

The sad irony for many who have such a deep need to keep things the same is that this very need can trigger an erratic life-style. This can be even more inconsistent and destructive than if they would just release themselves to normal life changes.

Hanging On No Matter What

Lisa is an adult child of divorce who has backed herself into a dangerous lifestyle because she insists on keeping things the same. She vowed to herself as a teenager that once one was married it was for life—no matter what. Her parents went through a nasty divorce when Lisa was ten and they dragged both their children along with them through many years of battle.

At thirty-two, Lisa vividly recalls the verbal abuse, sarcasm, innuendos, bitter tears, and sneaky plots. She remembers court hearings and custody suits, stepparents bickering with natural parents, dirty tricks being played back and forth between two households, and many sleepless nights. Lisa was *never* going to go through that!

Now Lisa is married to Tom, a drug abuser, who verbally assaults her, physically batters her, and sexually mauls her. But she will not consider leaving him — she married him for better or for worse.

I do not share Lisa's story to advocate divorce or to give guidelines about when a marriage is "bad enough" to make divorce okay. Rather, it is to reveal that there are times when staying together in an abusive situation "for the sake of consistency" can be very expensive — it may even cost people their lives in terms of the toll extracted from the physical, mental, emotional, and spiritual existence of the people involved.

There are times when it is healthier to step back, take a hard look at a situation, regroup, and seek help to make major changes in life to preserve sanity, stability, or life itself. Sometimes, a couple may need a time of separation to work through their marital and individual problems. Lisa and Tom's situation is a clear example of this.

One evening as Tom slammed out of the house and roared away in his car, Lisa became desperate. Tom had just pushed her into a corner of the china hutch and her head was bleeding. Their infant daughter was crying in her crib.

Lisa limped to the telephone to call her friend, Diane. This was not the first time Diane had received a call from Lisa in the middle of the night after Tom beat her. Diane could hear the baby crying in the background and sensed that things were serious. She told Lisa that she'd drive right over.

Then Lisa hung up the phone and collapsed on the floor. When Diane found her, Lisa was sobbing hysterically and shaking all over. Diane was outraged, "I'm going to call a doctor, Lisa," she shouted. "Hang on!"

Lisa curled into a ball and wailed, "Please! No! Diane, I'll be all right! Don't call a doctor!"

Diane was half repulsed and half engulfed in pity by Lisa's desperation. Something had to be done to help Lisa and Tom. Diane knew things had gone too far. She half-carried Lisa to the sofa.

"Come on, honey, let's see what the damage is this time." Diane could see blood oozing from a cut near Lisa's temple. She wet a cloth with warm water and carefully cleansed the area enough to see that the gash needed stitches.

"Lisa, you've got to see a doctor! This cut is deep and you need medical attention."

Lisa gulped for air between sobs and cried out, "Oh! Diane, please help! Tom—he—Tom raped me!"

Diane was blinded by an immediate rage. She trembled with emotion as she called her husband and told him briefly what had happened. He agreed to wait for Diane to drop Lisa's baby off on the way to the nearby hospital.

At the emergency room, Lisa refused to discuss with the doctor how she'd gotten the cut on her head. Diane stood helplessly by while Lisa refused to implicate Tom as being responsible for the cut on her head or to admit that he'd raped her.

In the hallway, Diane told the doctor bluntly that Tom was a drug abuser and what he'd done this evening. The doctor shook his head sadly. He said, "Unless you were an eye witness to what happened, or Lisa will admit these things and file charges against her husband, there's nothing I can do."

Diane stood with her mouth agape. What could she do? The doctor wouldn't keep Lisa in the hospital, Diane couldn't just drop her off at home as though everything was fine. She'd have to take Lisa home with her.

When they got to Diane's house, Diane tucked Lisa under blankets on the hide-a-bed, checked the sleeping baby, and crawled into bed herself. Diane couldn't fall asleep right away. She tried to think of what to do. How could she help Lisa to separate from Tom at least long enough to keep herself and the baby from immediate danger?

When morning came, Lisa was groggy and sullen. The whole side of her face was swollen and turning purple. Her eyes looked hollow and drained of emotion. She barely acknowledged Diane's presence as she sipped a glass of orange juice.

Diane's husband went to work. Diane called in to her office and took a personal day of absence. Then she sat across from Lisa at the table, took a deep breath, and said, "Lisa, we've got to deal with this."

Nobody Else Can Change or Choose for You

Lisa looked forlornly at Diane, "What's there to deal with? Tom was high, he raped me, and he beat me up. It's over. I'll need to get home soon or he'll be angry and do the same thing again."

Diane was astonished. "You're just going home and act like everything's dandy? Lisa, I can't let you do that!"

Lisa bristled, "Diane, Tom's my husband. I need to be at home. I'm grateful for your help and friendship, but there's nothing more you can do."

Diane's mind raced back and forth. On one hand, she wanted to shake Lisa to her senses and, on the other, to lock her upstairs in a room. They'd been over Lisa's reasoning for staying with Tom a hundred times before. Tom had been the only consistent thing in Lisa's life since she was sixteen when she had started dating him. He was there when Lisa's father refused to help pay for her yearbook at school because he said, "I already pay too much support!" Tom was there when Lisa's stepmother told the young woman what a brat and a burden she was to her father. Tom was there when Lisa's mother told Lisa she couldn't have a new dress for the prom because her father *didn't* pay enough child support. And Tom was there when Lisa's stepfather backhanded her for being sassy. In Lisa's eyes, Tom had always been there. Her deep need for consistency was too great a bondage for her to be able to see things differently.

In the end, Diane had no real choice but to take Lisa and her baby home. After hours of pleading and trying to convince Lisa to go to a shelter for battered women, or to a doctor, or to a counselor or social service agency — anywhere for help — Lisa still held firm. Tom was her husband and she would stick by him.

That evening Diane was so upset that her husband stepped in where he hadn't before. He told Diane he didn't want her to go to Lisa's rescue anymore. He said that without Diane to bail her out of a crisis she would be forced to seek professional help. Diane was depressed. She knew instinctively that her husband was right. But what if Tom *killed* Lisa?

Diane's husband said that next time Lisa asked them for help they could offer to summon the police to her aid, but they could not ruin their own family life or enable Lisa to continue to live with such violence anymore. Diane agreed.

A few weeks later, Lisa called Diane again in the middle of the night. This time Tom had been smashing glasses from a cabinet against the fireplace and Lisa got cut when she tried to stop him. She was sobbing for Diane to come help.

Diane gritted her teeth and said kindly that she could call the police if Lisa wanted her to, but she couldn't keep rushing over at all hours only to bring Lisa back to the same hell the next day. Lisa needed more help than Diane could give.

Lisa was crushed. In her mind this was nothing more than another desertion. Diane was no better than her parents and stepparents. Again, Tom was the only one there.

Eventually, Lisa had no say in the matter anyway. While Tom was in a drug-induced stupor he brought a woman home and had her wait in the living room while he packed his belongings. After calling Lisa all sorts of vulgar names he left with the woman.

Lisa went on welfare and started to depend on alcohol to numb her frazzled nerves. Her baby was neglected to the point that a neighbor reported Lisa to Social Services and the youngster was taken into protective custody. Lisa was allowed to visit her child only in a foster home. The last Diane heard about Lisa through the grapevine was that she was living in a cheap motel room in a sleazy part of town.

Emotional Development Arrested

Lisa's case study is an extreme example of how horribly the effects of divorce can influence a young child's development and later life. Lisa never grew emotionally beyond the stage of childhood. She was an adult woman trapped under the heavy burden of a Piggy-Back Child. This Piggy-Back Child suffocated any of the normal resources Lisa would otherwise have learned to cope with severe crises as an adult. Lisa never understood the basics of taking responsibility for her own life. To her, Tom in any way, shape, or form was better than nothing. He left a wife who was like a ten-year-old child, to raise herself with no support system. Lisa was dying a slow and agonizing death. She never knew that the so-called consistency she leaned on so heavily for survival was actually the *inconsistent* type of behavior that kept her emotionally enmeshed with her Piggy–Back Child.

Not every ACD clings so tightly to such abusive and unhealthy situations, of course. There can be, however, a great need for unhealthy consistency that rises up and definitely inhibits other areas of life, stifling growth and opportunities.

When Change Threatens

Maryann's life clicked along at a frighteningly smooth pace. She got up at the same time each day, played out the same routines, and went to bed at the same hour every night month after month, year after year. About the biggest inconsistency in her life was to host or attend periodic family gatherings throughout the year. However, even the holiday meals shared with family produced anxiety in her because she needed consistency so badly. There was no room in her life for surprises, which, of course, meant she had no life.

You can imagine then what turmoil she felt one weekday afternoon when her husband, Dale, arrived home from work to announce quietly that he'd received notice from his boss that very day. He was to be transferred to his company's headquarters two thousand miles away.

Maryann nearly fainted. Her heart pounded frantically, her palms grew clammy, and her breathing came in short gasps. This couldn't really be happening to her! Immediately she started thinking of ways to get out of the move she knew her husband's transfer would require. Of all the major life changes that would have unnerved Maryann, moving was *the worst!*

Maryann had grown up in a military family. They moved to different places periodically. Just as Maryann was ready to enter junior high her parents announced they were going to divorce. To make the nightmare worse, Maryann's mother was being shipped overseas for three years and her father was staying stateside.

After an agonizing week of tearful discussions, it was decided that Maryann and her brother, who had two years left of high school, would stay with their father. Maryann was so upset she vomited and had diarrhea for several hours the day her mother left for Germany.

The broken family limped along the next two years with Maryann's father doing the best he could to run the household, guide his children, participate in his career, and put the pieces of his personal life together again. Maryann was left alone for long hours while her brother and father socialized or worked. She was lonely and depressed much of the time. Her mother visited the children twice in two years—at Christmas when there were lots of other friends and relatives visiting or calling at all hours.

After Maryann married Dale, the lifestyle they planned seemed a perfect antidote for Maryann's great need for consistent love and a stable environment. Dale was a young salesman who wanted to work his way up through the ranks of a large corporation. He purposely asked to be assigned to a region of the country where it appeared he could stay his entire career.

Maryann dealt with the major life events she and Dale encountered with seemingly great aplomb. The moves they shared from an apartment to a suburban development within the same city, and finally to an upper middle-class neighborhood, didn't seem to bother her too much. She could still get up at the same time, make coffee in the same pot, go to the same bank, purchase groceries in the same store, and buy gas at the same station. Even if it was a little out of her way to drive to her old haunts, the security was worth it.

Maryann handled the birth of her only child pretty well, too. Stacy was a symbol of roots and consistency to Maryann. Lots of the changes involved with parenthood unsettled Maryann, but none that weren't worth the effort in order to create the "perfect," consistent homelife she so desperately wanted.

Ten years went by. Dale became a vice president of sales and marketing. Stacy was a model fourth-grader. Maryann seemed to have achieved a perfect environment. The only bumps in her path were occasional visits from her parents and their respective spouses. These visits derailed Maryann emotionally. Her parents' presence still reminded her of the days when nothing in her life felt consistent—the times she didn't know when she would see her mother again, when her father or brother might get home, what she was going to eat for supper, or who her father might bring home to spend the night. The feelings that Maryann experienced during this time in her life were lodged tightly somewhere between her stomach and her head. They still lived in the heart of the Piggy-Back Child she carried around her neck and on her back.

When she was around her parents, all the old emotions felt brand new. Thankfully, her parents didn't visit very often. And when they did, Dale was especially supportive and understanding. During these times Maryann survived the anxiety attacks and stomachaches with Dale's help.

But out of the ashes of her childhood nightmares arose the specter of threat to her consistency—Dale's transfer meant a move away from what Maryann saw as the very foundation of her life. She was thrown into such a strong emotional turbulence that she didn't leave her house for four days. When she finally did, her stomach was queasy, she cried as she drove down the familiar streets, and her pulse pounded wildly at her temples. Maryann didn't think she could make it.

Dale was deeply concerned about Maryann's state of mind. He didn't know whether to get medical help or just leave her alone. He considered turning down the transfer. But that would mean being demoted to the position of training salesmen and risking never being offered another transfer or promotion again.

As Dale struggled with thoughts of how to help Maryann and what was best to do, Maryann grappled with her emotions. Intellectually, she knew a major move would not kill her, but her emotions caused her body to feel as though it might.

Management: Dealing with Change

From the moment of birth we all undergo one long process of change called life. There is nothing at all that we can do to stop it. Year passes year, one after the other, and most of us grow from infants to toddlers to children to teens to adults, and develop to some degree, until we reach old age. Then we are birthed from this world via death into the next world — eternity.

We have no control over many of our life changes. Who can stop a normal baby from learning to walk? Who can prevent a healthy child who attends school from learning? Who can command a young woman's period not to start or a young man's voice not to change? There are multitudes of changes in our lives that we don't fight because we assume them to be normal or unavoidable. Many may frighten us somewhat, but we generally accept these.

Then there are changes we can see are coming, sense we have no real control over, wish we did, and try to avert. What father hasn't wished he could hold back the hands of time and try (even if only for a little while) to slow the accelerating pace of his child's growing up? What woman hasn't seen the first gray hairs or tiny wrinkles and tried to impede the aging process with hair color, moisturizer, vitamins, or plastic surgery?

This is the kind of change divorce often presents to families. Even if both spouses want the divorce with equal earnestness, their children usually do not want this alternative in their lives. They often try their best to thwart this change!

ACDs have all kinds of stories about how they tried to stop their parents from getting a divorce and how they tried (some for several years) to get their parted parents back together. Little Ann cooked up false stories of one parent who supposedly wanted to get back together and related them to the other parent. Tim told his parents he thought he had an incurable disease and since he was probably going to die, couldn't they stay together until afterward? Dean found a way to tell most of his mother's dates that his parents were talking about getting back together any day. Tawyna asked her teacher to tell her parents that she would flunk the fifth grade if they got divorced. David suffered silently through all kinds of imaginary plots to keep his parents from divorcing — until he got an ulcer shortly after his ninth birthday.

Many extraordinary methods are used by children to *stop the change and keep the status quo*, usually no matter how miserable that may be. They want life to remain consistent!

Thousands upon thousands of children whose parents are divorcing or divorced go through problems with schoolwork, social development, sleep disturbances, emotional outbursts or withdrawal, disciplinary challenges, and physical illness. Their small minds, bodies, and hearts instinctively try to stop the tidal wave of change that is crashing their lives to pieces.

Years later, as adult children of divorce, these same minds, bodies, and hearts may react very similarly to other undesired life changes — just as Maryann did to her impending move.

As Maryann and Dale fretted over what to do about Maryann's negative reactions to the move, the time to go loomed closer and closer. Maryann sensed she really couldn't stop this life change any more than she could have stopped her parents' divorce.

Forcing Yourself from the "Comfortable Zone"

One day, a neighbor down the block whom Maryann had not met called to her as Maryann was taking her usual morning walk. Maryann stopped and the woman walked across her yard and extended a hand.

"Hi! I'm Olivia!" she said. "Are you the lady whose house is for sale up the street?"

Maryann felt a familiar tightness in her chest as she nodded.

"Oh," Olivia grinned, "well, where are you off to?"

Maryann felt the excitement in Olivia's voice and couldn't help but be curious — who could be so happy about a move? She answered, "My husband is being transferred to the west coast."

"Ooh!" Olivia lit up, "Where?! California?!"

"Yes," Maryann nodded again.

"How thrilling! I bet you can't wait to get out of Kansas City!" Olivia exclaimed.

Maryann bristled, "Not at all! I don't want to leave here — ever!"

Olivia's face fell, "Oh, I'm sorry."

Maryann was embarrassed at being short with the open-faced young woman. "No, that's all right. I'm just a little emotional right now because I don't want to move."

Olivia brightened. More cautiously she asked, "Would you like to come in for tea?"

Maryann felt a little obligated, "Okay."

As Olivia put water on for tea, Maryann looked around her colorful kitchen. It was warm and welcoming. For the first time in weeks Maryann felt herself relax a little.

The two made small talk for a brief time and then Olivia asked bluntly, "Why don't you want to leave here?"

Maryann was taken off guard, "Because I'm used to here."

"Don't you get bored with the same place and routine?" Olivia queried.

"No," Maryann replied, "I like my life to be consistent. Besides, I moved around a lot when I was a kid. Plus my parents got divorced."

Olivia looked confused, "What does that have to do with anything?"

Maryann hadn't thought before making the statement, but Olivia's question stirred something inside her. She answered,

"I don't know, I guess it made me not like big changes very much."

"Oh." Olivia looked puzzled. "I love change. I don't always quite know how to work things out, but I try to figure stuff so I can make things happen."

"Like what?" Maryann was more curious now.

"Oh, like how to be able to afford to live on my husband's salary so I can quit my nursing job and have a baby. Or how to arrange things so I can go back to school in a couple years to become a doctor. Stuff like that. Whenever we find ourselves in a 'Comfortable Zone' my husband and I always force ourselves out of it and on to the next phase of our lives."

"You do?" Maryann was incredulous. Here was a woman several years younger than she who welcomed, even went out of her way, to orchestrate major changes in her life.

"Oh, yes!" Olivia beamed. "You know, all of life is one string of change anyway — why not get behind the ball and push it instead of always trying to run away from it?"

Maryann was intrigued. She'd spent her whole life accepting the changes she couldn't avoid and fighting those she knew probably couldn't be prevented. Now here was someone who was eager for change. Maryann felt the slightest tingle of hope move somewhere deep in her stomach.

"I bet you wouldn't just up and move from here," she challenged Olivia.

"Oh, yes I would!" Olivia shot back. "I'd be outta here in a heartbeat if my husband was transferred again. We came here two years ago from Rhode Island. Two years before that we were in Louisiana. I'd like to go to Hawaii!"

"I see." Maryann was subdued. "You're awfully adventuresome. Doesn't it scare you to pick up your household and move everything — your whole lives — somewhere else?"

"Sure, it scares the socks off me!" Olivia answered honestly. "But if we don't do things that scare us sometimes we don't get very much living done."

"I guess that's true," Maryann acknowledged. "I'm scared of almost everything outside of my daily habits."

"Well, maybe you're just not giving yourself a fair shake," Olivia offered. "Maybe you just need to stick your neck out of the 'Comfortable Zone' and go with the change no matter what it feels like."

Just the thought of actually moving made Maryann anxious. So far, she'd managed to ward off every house showing the realtors tried to arrange in hopes that if the house didn't sell they wouldn't have to move. The thought of voluntarily putting the move together made her nauseated.

"Hey!" Olivia said excitedly, "I know — we can role play your move and practice how it will feel for you. You said your parents' divorce made you not like change very much. But you know, their divorce is over and done with. It doesn't have to stop you from moving out of your 'Comfortable Zone' now. Let's pretend that you feel neutral about your move and have a walk-through of the whole procedure."

Maryann balked at what she saw as silly. "I think I should be going. Thank you anyway."

Olivia looked hurt, "Okay. Well, if you change your mind just let me know. I'll be happy to practice with you."

Maryann went home with a heavy heart. She tried to envelope herself into her comfortable cocoon of consistency, but she couldn't keep her mind on her usual routine. The fresh, joyful neighbor down the block had opened doors in Maryann's world that just wouldn't close. Maryann even tried shutting all her drapes and blinds. Maybe the half-darkness would soothe the far-off roar she felt inside her.

It was too late. For the next two days, Maryann was tormented by thoughts of actually packing up her belongings and physically seeing them off in a moving van. She had visions of calling utility companies to shut off services in Kansas City and turn them on in San Francisco. Her stomach knotted and ached.

On the third day, Maryann couldn't bring herself to get out of bed. She hurt all over. She told Dale she just had whatever virus the warm, moist spring had brought. But inside she admitted she was paralyzed by the mounting fear that she would actually have to go through with the move.

Maryann napped on and off all day. Late in the afternoon she awoke with a clear remembrance from her childhood. She and her visiting grandmother had been shopping for a dress for Maryann's fourth grade play. Maryann's grandmother bought a small gift for a family next door to her that had just adopted their fifth child. Maryann knew the couple was very poor and she'd asked her grandmother, "Why do the Barretts keep getting more kids? I heard you tell Mom they couldn't even buy their daughter new shoes — she had to wear worn out ones from one of the older kids."

If God Asks, It Can't Be Wrong!

Maryann's grandmother had taken Maryann's hand and said, "Honey, when God asks us to trust Him by moving from one plateau in life to the next, we'd better hustle. If He asks us to do something, it can't be wrong — no matter what it looks like."

Maryann recalled that she'd asked her grandmother how to tell if God was asking a person to do something. It was as if her grandmother were right there in the bedroom, answering her, "You know God's asking when you've prayed for an answer to a problem, when you've talked it over with those involved and others you trust, when you've thought it through inside out and upside down, read the Bible for examples of similar situations, felt in your middle it was right, and it just won't go away!"

That afternoon, for the first time since her parents' divorce, Maryann knelt down and prayed. The next morning she got up earlier than usual, anxious to send Dale off to work and get Stacy off to school. When both were gone, Maryann walked briskly to Olivia's front door before she lost her nerve.

Olivia smiled widely when she saw it was Maryann. She said, "I thought I might see you here again."

For the next week, Olivia helped Maryann "practice" moving in her mind. One day Maryann was pretending to call the moving company and she burst into tears. As the tears streamed down her face, she was emotionally back to the place where she'd overheard her mother calling a friend to bring his pick-up truck to help her move her things out of the house and into storage.

Another time Olivia made a casual remark about writing a list of any furniture to sell and Maryann shouted in anger, "No way! I'm not selling even one of my possessions!"

Maryann suddenly realized that in more than a decade of marriage she hadn't gotten rid of a single piece of furniture, clothing, or anything else that she could store in an attic, basement, or garage. She needed consistency so badly that to sell or give away any possession represented giving away a part of herself.

After a week of practice, Maryann was able to let realtors show her home. She inwardly dreaded the time someone would present an offer, but she had made up her mind to take one day at a time.

The day came that Maryann had to stare at the cold, black and white print of a purchase agreement for the house. Her signature was the only one of four missing. Her heart thudded so hard in her chest she was sure the realtor and Dale heard it. She kept pretending to read the agreement over more closely all the while she was trying to collect her emotions.

Maryann went over all the mental "support clauses" she and Olivia had practiced—there would be another house to make a home; home is where you create your own safe place; the move was good for Dale; it would be a healthy adventure for Stacy; and Maryann would grow beyond her "Comfortable Zone" to higher plateaus.

Dale watched Maryann closely. He was so grateful to Olivia for her help and support. He'd just about given up hope that Maryann would be able to cope with the move. Then the emotional chains that held her in bondage began to break one by one. Dale realized now that he was holding his breath. He knew that this was the telling moment. If Maryann could bring herself to sign the agreement, there would be no going back—the offer to buy was a sound one.

Slowly, ever so slowly, Maryann fingered the pen on the table. She picked it up. She put one end in her mouth and chewed on it. She tapped the fingers of her left hand on the table. Dale saw her flush red. Then, all of a sudden, it was over — Maryann signed the agreement and slapped the pen down.

"There!" she cried, "I did it! We're going to move!"

There Is One Thing That Never Changes

The next weeks were a blur of activity. There were times when Maryann felt as though she'd be swallowed up by her anxieties and fears. But she faithfully put one foot in front of the other. Dale's support on one side and Olivia's on the other held her up when she would have fallen.

Moving day arrived. Maryann started shaking as soon as she woke up, even before she opened her eyes. She lay in bed, praying, begging God to help her get through the day. Finally, she got up and began the final phase of her passage. Several hours later, the moving van was gone, all their good-byes had been said and Dale turned the key in the lock of the front door for the last time.

In the car, on the way to the closing of escrow, Dale turned to Maryann, "What gave you the courage to sign the purchase agreement that day?"

Maryann's eyes filled with tears as she answered, "The ultimate consistency — it says in Hebrews 13:8 that 'Jesus Christ is the same yesterday and today and forever.'"

As an adult child of divorce, you may very well have a great need for consistency in your life. You may meet this need in little, eccentric ways, such as always using the same kind of soap or brand of coffee. On the other hand, you may have paralyzing fears of change, such as Maryann did. You may even be affected so destructively that you are living in a life-threatening situation as Lisa was. And there are different kinds of effects that range all through these examples.

There are three main things to remember, as Maryann learned, when you are trying to monitor or break your resistance to change:

1. Bear in mind that from the moment of birth, your life is one long process of change and transformation.

2. Accept the fact that it is usually necessary and beneficial to force yourself from your own "Comfortable Zone" periodically in order to participate in or initiate healthy changes in your life.

3. Remember that if you feel God is asking you to make a major life change and you've prayed, talked, thought, and read the Bible about it — and it still won't "let go of you" — then most likely it isn't wrong!

One way to "practice" a change mentally that is threatening to you is to use metaphors. The following exercise offers instructions on how to do this.

Exercise: Practicing Change with Metaphors

Change can be very difficult to implement for anyone. It can be devastatingly hard for adult children of divorce who have a great need for consistency. By creating your own versions of the following examples of practicing change with metaphors, you may help to alleviate some of the pressure and anxiety of change:

Else, forty-three, could not bring herself to break out of the grip of anxiety each time she tried to get herself to register for college courses. She had been a housewife and mother all her adult life and leaving behind her safe lifestyle of the past really frightened her. But Else used metaphors to help her change, to help her gain the courage she needed to get into college. Here's how:

Else was fifteen when her parents divorced. She was very vocal about her disapproval of and disgust for her parents' decision and many of their behaviors. They used to tell Else, "Shut up, girl! You're just too smart for your own good!"

Else now used this cutting remark as an inspiration for her metaphor and imagining. "Smart" to Else related to books and books related to college. So, each day for several weeks, Else would sit quietly in a chair and close her eyes. She would mentally envision a whole covey of college textbooks lined up neatly on her kitchen table. Then Else envisioned that one-by-one, the books got wings and fluttered around her kitchen.

Else loved to watch butterflies fluttering just as the books did in her imagination. And, as a young girl, Else remembered thinking how much fun it would be to be tiny enough to fly away on a butterfly's back. In Else's metaphoric imaging, the books were "smart," and their flight was "freedom," just as the butterflies represented freedom when she was a child. The only element left was to get into a position of feeling the "freedom to get smart."

She envisioned herself getting tiny and flying freely off to college to get smart. When she arrived she imagined she saw the flying books land in neat stacks on a big table in the library where, in her mind's eye, Else was transformed into an adult student studying for an exam.

When Else awakened the morning she was actually to register for college, her stomach felt like it was chock full of her fluttering butterflies! But she replayed her vision again and again as she got ready, drove to the campus, walked into the registrar's office, and even as she filled out her papers. When she was finished, Else walked around the grounds, found the library and with a smile on her face, went in to explore it.

Else had to use the metaphoric imagining to get through her anxiety every day for the first few weeks of school. But eventually she only needed it periodically. Now, Else is nearly two years into college and loves it—she's made the dean's list every quarter!

Brad used a different type of metaphor to free himself from the bondage of some heavy-duty obligations he desperately wanted to get away from but kept because "that's the way he'd always done things."

Brad was greatly overburdened when his parents divorced. He was ten at the time and his mother let him know immediately that he was "the man of the house." Brad took his role very seriously. He loved his mother and he wanted her to be proud of him and not cry anymore.

So little Brad washed the car, took out the garbage, fed the animals, mowed the lawn, pulled weeds, painted the house trim, raked leaves, swept the garage, and did everything he could possibly manage to do while he grew up. He stayed at home during college and continued to "take good care of his mother."

When Brad married, he and his new bride lived in the same town as his mother. He continued to take care of her, took on the maintenance of his own home and also fell into a crippling role as "everybody's helper" at work and with friends. By the time Brad and his wife had two half-grown daughters, Brad's days, nights, and weekends were so full of helping commitments that he was completely stressed-out.

Brad used imagery with metaphors to extract himself from the consistent role he'd assumed since childhood. After he got home from work, Brad pulled the window shades in his room, closed the door, and lay still on his bed. He envisioned himself to be a small puppy trapped in a net. As a puppy, he would chew through one strand of netting at a time. As each strand snapped, one of Brad's responsibilities would also "snap" and be gone — until there was a big enough hole in the net (enough responsibilities gone) to set him free.

Then the puppy could run out and romp around the yard, play freely as the young boy, Brad, couldn't do. Brad's Piggy-Back Child was liberated! Slowly, one by one, Brad eliminated or delegated his obligations in real life until he had enough free time to play golf and tennis and even watch an old movie on Saturday afternoon television once in awhile.

Metaphors can be a wonderfully fun and freeing experience for anyone, but especially so for ACDs who are trying to integrate their Piggy-Back Children with their adult selves and get loose from consistencies that hold them back from healthy change!

You may envision yourself to be a flower growing in the warm sun, a balloon floating on a gentle breeze, or a sailboat setting out to sea. Let yourself change in your mind and you may be surprised at what a powerful step this is to help you change something in reality.

##

One of the most propelling forces in the lives of ACDs is often a constant, underlying fear of abandonment that influences — consciously or subconsciously — nearly every life decision they make. We will look at this abiding fear closely in the next chapter and examine various ways to cope with it.

-6-

The Fear of Abandonment

Bryan distinctly remembers the day his parents split up. He was seven and he thought life was wonderful — until he padded out to the kitchen to get a bowl of cereal for breakfast one sunny morning. He describes what happened, "When we woke up one morning my dad was just gone — packed and gone. Mom sort of grumbled at us while we got ready for school, telling us to hurry up, things would work themselves out. She sent us off to meet the day as though nothing unusual had happened!

"My whole world fell around my ankles like a baggy pair of trousers, and I was expected to go to school feeling stark naked and do just fine!

"I remember my younger sister slept with my mom for weeks after my dad left. But my older brother and I toughed the whole thing out alone in our bunkbeds each night. I'd lay there, staring up at the springs holding my brother's mattress, and wonder which one of us kids did something so rotten that our dad had to move away from home."

Bryan's face pinches and grows white as he continues: "Nobody ever bothered to let us know that the divorce was between my mom and dad—not between them and us kids.

"Looking back, I'm sure my mom and dad were too devastated themselves to cope with us kids being emotional bowls of jelly. But all I knew was that I'd been abandoned—physically and emotionally."

Bryan's mother, Nel, relates how it was for her. "I felt so guilty and worthless that I couldn't really discuss the whole situation with the kids. It was as if I'd failed everyone in my life—my parents, my in-laws, myself, my husband, and my children. I was so afraid to impose my emotional chaos on my children that it was easier to avoid saying anything. I just kept telling them things would work out, thinking this would give them some semblance of comfort.

"However, I guess I was wrong; all three of my children grew up with deeply rooted fears of abandonment. Bryan, his sister, and I have been in counseling together for nearly two years now, and I'm truly amazed at how the kids' reality became so distorted."

Denial and Distortion

Nel continues, "The kids grew up with a strong belief that their dad simply abandoned them physically and that I abandoned them emotionally. Hearing them put their childhood fears and memories into adult words I realize now that I suffered a great deal of denial after the divorce. I didn't want to confront and cope with the fury I felt at the unexpected turn my life had taken, or the hellish spot it put my children in."

Bryan comments, "From an adult's perspective, kids may distort reality, but it's important to remember that, to them, whatever they're thinking or feeling at the time is reality. This reality sort of sticks to them and rides on their backs into adulthood. To me, reliving the day my dad left home can feel as real as it did then. I can put names to the feelings now, is all.

"You can't explain to a seven-year-old that there's a difference between his dad leaving the family and *abandoning* the family. You have to work and work with that child, like a sculptor with clay, until the boy feels more secure and can trust again.

"If the divorcing parents deny the tremendous impact their choices have on their children, it makes the children's fear of being abandoned grow and grow until it affects everything they do. I'm thirty now, and I've been in counseling most of my adult life trying to sort through all of the trauma my Piggy–Back Child experienced and carried along with me into adulthood.

"I have a lovely wife, Cindy, and a great three-year-old son, Peter. I can't tell you how terrorized I am sometimes by nightmares of Cindy leaving me and taking Peter away! I've had to consciously face my fears that they would abandon me and work on my insecurities in counseling. I became so obsessed that Cindy might abandon me that I decided I would be the perfect husband and father so she would have no reason to leave. I became such a perfectionist, however, that I did just the opposite—I alienated Cindy and nearly drove her to leave me!

"I set such high standards for myself that she couldn't possibly be interdependent with me. I gave her no choice but to either become codependent and feed into my need to have a perfect life or withdraw from me to live her own life.

"For instance, I demanded that we keep an exact, to-the-minute schedule each day. We had to work this schedule and I would tolerate no exceptions. We had a perfectly maintained household, yard, cars, and relationship.

"I made sure that we 'kept' our relationship to the letter. All my years of counseling provided an excellent opportunity to exercise my communication and problem-solving skills to 'perfection.' Actually, I abused the technical skills and used them to manipulate Cindy. I forced her to talk to death every little issue in our lives so our relationship would supposedly stay healthy.

"There was no room in my life for blemishes. We overdiscussed everything, from how Cindy arranged the throw pillows on our bed to why she chose a particular brand of polish for our furniture!" Bryan shakes his head.

Pushing Loved Ones Away

Bryan continues, "Cindy felt so pressured by my expectations and the structured lives we were living that I drove her away emotionally. I began to feel abandoned, as I did with my mom after dad left home. That really panicked me!

"Pretty soon I didn't even want Cindy to leave me alone. If I was home, I wanted her there too. If I found myself alone even for a few minutes I'd begin worrying about the smallest things, such as where to plant the new rosebush, or what kind of shoes we should buy for Peter, or when we would plan next week's menus. I would become such a bundle of nerves that I'd blow up at the least word or action from Cindy that differed from my way of thinking.

"Eventually, Cindy couldn't take it anymore. She started challenging me. We began arguing excessively. I suggested that she come to counseling with me. That completely shook her up. In her mind, counseling was screwing me up, not helping me. In reality, my deep fear of abandonment had not been brought to the surface yet and I was acting it out at home instead of working through it.

"Anyhow, Cindy refused to go to counseling with me. We kept arguing and I began to fear, after every argument, that she would pack her bags and leave—like my dad did."

Dread of Partings

Bryan clasps his hands and looks off into space, as if to some distant place. He says, "Cindy is such a wonderful person. I wanted not to lose her so badly that I almost did. The turning point came when she caught on—by accident—what the real issue was with me.

"My brother and his family visited us from the West Coast for two weeks about a year ago. The first week was terrific. We did tourist things and talked late into the night. The second week began fine, too. I loved having them at the house. Cindy noticed that for the first seven or eight days I nearly let go of my rigid schedule and relaxed for the first time in months, even years.

"Then, when the time got closer for them to leave, I started grasping at my same old patterns again. I put us back on our schedule and orchestrated the last of my brother's visit like a drill sergeant. The day before my brother and his family left I was especially irritable and anxious. I couldn't sleep that night, and my tossing woke up Cindy. She took me in her arms and asked, 'Bryan, why do you think you dread your brother's leaving so intensely?'

"I told her that I didn't, I just had a lot on my mind and couldn't sleep. But saying good-bye the next day was so hard on me I could hardly get through it. I actually went for a ride alone after they left and cried. I was so heartbroken and depressed.

"I brought up the incident in counseling the next week because I was still feeling let down and anxious. My counselor asked me why I thought separating from my brother affected me so deeply. I didn't have an answer. But I thought back to Cindy's question about dreading my brother's leaving, and I realized she was right. I did dread it. In fact, I realized that I dread all good-byes of any kind. I related this to the counselor and described how I'd felt just before other partings in my life.

"I remember leaving home after high school and feeling physically ill. When Cindy and I were first married I had to go out of town on a business trip. As I said good-bye to Cindy I wanted to run back into the house and hide under the covers! Even saying, 'So long,' after a holiday spent with my family or Cindy's makes my stomach nervous.

"The counselor bluntly asked me, 'Do you think that when you say good-bye to loved ones it's a kind of abandonment, either you leaving them or them leaving you, just as you were abandoned as a child?'"

Reliving the Moment

Bryan looks desolate as he relives the morning he awoke to find his father gone. He explains his adult dread of parting.

"Over a period of several weeks I came to realize that hearing my loved ones say good-bye to me as I deliberately left them was like replaying my dad's leaving. I felt the way I imagined I would've felt if I'd had a chance to say good-bye to my dad. And every time I separated from someone I cared about I felt threatened that they might never come back into my life again.

"You see, my dad didn't say good-bye to me when he left the house, he just went. And even though I saw him again it was in a different house in another town. Then he acted as if everything was 'normal,' the way it used to be. But it never was again. I guess I picked up such a bizarre idea of what was 'normal' about separating from others that my Piggy–Back Child still reacted with skepticism, dread, and fear, even though my adult mind knew the parting was not a permanent thing like my parents' divorce."

As Bryan contemplates his process of becoming used to good-byes and easing his fear of abandonment he notes that making headway is slower because he never had a chance to actually tell his father good-bye when he left. This has caused Bryan anguish from two different angles.

"On the one hand," Bryan explains, "I didn't get to experience the feeling of physical separation, of watching my dad leave. But on the other, my fear of being abandoned like that again has come out in a dread of saying good-bye and deliberately parting from any of my loved ones.

"My dad died about four years ago in an auto accident. In many ways it was like going through his leaving our family all over again. The shock, grief, helplessness, and mourning felt the same."

Grief and Mourning

Bryan shrugs and says, "Even though the odds are against it happening again, once you've experienced abandonment you always know it could happen again. Anyone who hasn't gone through parental abandonment as a child or the death of a close loved one cannot understand the dread and fear you live with that there could be a repeat performance. Kids who never experience abandonment or death of a person close to them live more securely and peacefully than those of us who are haunted with the prospect that we could be left again."

Disturbed Sleep

"I was abandoned twice by the same person in less than twenty years. How are those odds?" Bryan runs his hand over his head. "I was devastated when I lost my dad again. I began to have incredible nightmares about my mom dying, Cindy leaving, and me being left all alone in the world. They got so bad that I tried not to fall asleep. Of course, I did sleep finally, but sometimes I'd wake up with my heart pounding and a dreadful feeling of loss.

"My counselor told me it was common to have disturbed sleep as both a child and an adult of divorce. Nightmares, sleeplessness, grinding teeth, sleep-walking, talking, or shouting out during sleep, and physical tension were all things his clients of divorce have described.

"About the time Peter was born I began to be able periodically to sleep through the night again. But when we brought Peter home I was a mess from worrying that something would happen to him. I'd frequently sit in a rocking chair near his crib and sleep sitting up, I guess in an attempt to protect him. Sometimes I'd stand over his crib and literally tell this tiny creature that he didn't have to worry, I'd never leave him. After a while, though, I began to consider that Cindy could leave me and take Peter with her. He would never know of my vow to stick by him until it was too late and the damage was done and he had already felt the pain of abandonment."

Professional Counseling

Bryan's life has been riddled with twists and turns of anxieties, fears, dreads, worries, and unanswered questions that were little more than seedling weeds during and after his parents' divorce. The seedlings grew, however, until they nearly choked out normal growth. His fear of abandonment, grief after his father's death, and an irrational drive to make his family life perfect nearly caused the very thing he tried to avoid — another parting, this time of his wife and child.

Cindy tells her side, "I was so fed up with Bryan's morbid preoccupation with having the perfect household and family life that, more than once, I almost left him. But I could see that emotionally he was a poor little child. After the incident when his brother left to go home and Bryan had to work through those feelings with the help of counseling, I could see clearly that my leaving him was his worst dread.

"I began to work on interacting with him instead of reacting to him. I found my own counselor about a year ago and started working on really breaking down the emotional barriers I'd built up between Bryan and me as I withdrew from him more and more.

"Bryan, his mom, and his sister go together to Bryan's counselor once a month to work through their problems that stem from the past. Bryan goes on his own once a month. I still go bi-weekly. Not everyone has such intricate problems that they require so much intensive counseling, but ours is one family that highly recommends at least some kind of professional help for a family network overcoming the effects of divorce. There are just too many feelings, fears, and questions left unanswered in many divorced families. And those who marry into disturbed networks, unaware of all the underground issues that control the way family interacts, need all the help they can get!"

Cindy rolls her eyes upward. "I don't know where I'd be if I hadn't found a good counselor. Things are far from perfect in our lives, but we're getting better all the time. Bryan is better able to put his feelings into words and to put his problems in perspective. All his relationships are more meaningful. I'm learning how to love Bryan as he is each step of the way and not absorb his problems into myself. One of Bryan's most stubborn issues is still a fear of abandonment. Just last week he dreamed that Peter and I escaped from danger across a river and left him stranded on the opposite bank."

Of all the relationship issues Adult Children of Divorce face, fear of abandonment can be one of the most difficult to handle because it can prompt or greatly magnify all the others: dysfunctional relationships, frenzied living, tendency toward extremes, insecurity, great need for consistency, low self-esteem, loneliness, physical ailments, feelings of being cheated out of happiness, and a desire to control.

MANAGEMENT: LEARNING TO TRUST

There are two overlapping issues involved with the agonizing fear of abandonment and a distinct need to learn or re-learn how to trust both yourself and others:

1. Betrayal
2. Loyalty

The ultimate human trust relationship is surely that between parent and child. From the moment of birth, a little one instinctively trusts its parent for its very survival.

There are classic tales of social service agencies advising courts to remove children from parental custody for all sorts of hideous abuses. Yet, the children from these homes beg to stay with their parents regardless of what is being done to them. This is one of the most warped examples of misplaced trust. But if all a child knows from his parents is abuse, it becomes something consistent, a familiarity the child can rely on. When parents break family trust with the child by divorcing, a gap is left in the child's ego that will need particular care to fill in and repair. This child's sense of loyalty, no matter what his circumstances at home, has been betrayed. He can no longer trust his parents. From a child's viewpoint the issue can be that simple — abandonment by any means is devastating.

Betrayal

Tracy, twenty-seven, remembers how she felt when her parents divorced. She was fourteen and felt so betrayed she hated them both with a vengeance. She describes her emotions: "I was so filled with anger and resentment toward my parents that I threw every single one of my hundred or more record albums on my bedroom floor and stomped them to pieces."

Tracy's jaw clenches as she continues, "I cannot put into words how deeply enraged I was when the two most important people in my life—the people I'd trusted all my life to clothe, feed, shelter, and care for me emotionally—flaked out. No matter how furious I got with them at times, I trusted my parents with my life. And they betrayed that trust! When I began to date I was determined not to trust any male—ever! The anger and sense of betrayal I felt over my parents' split was still too raw.

"I met Alan in college. I felt myself falling head over heels in love with him and fought it every step of the way. I dated him time after time. All the while I tried to convince myself it was a casual thing. If he was late picking me up by a couple of minutes, or I discovered him somewhere other than where he said he was going to be at a certain time, I would loudly point out to him how I couldn't trust him and how he'd betrayed me.

"Over a period of several months Alan and I got thicker and thicker. We shared our backgrounds and dreams for the future with each other. But I still didn't fully trust him. Inside, I waited for the fall to come, the time when he'd betray and then abandon me."

Tracy looks sheepish as she goes on. "One night I was going back to my dorm with a group of girls. As we came from the library I saw Alan give this girl a huge hug. I freaked out! I ran up to him and started hollering about how I'd been right about him all along. As soon as he got a chance to betray me, he did! Oh, I was so angry. It was as if I were yelling at my parents all over again.

"When there was a pause for Alan to speak, he said, 'Lynn, this is the great girl I've been telling you about, Tracy. Tracy, meet Lynn, my sister.' I could have crawled into a manhole," Tracy exclaims.

Give Loyalty a Chance

"Later," Tracy continues, "Alan and I talked the whole thing through. He told me he understood my skepticism, mistrust, fear of betrayal, and of abandonment. He said that's why he hadn't tried to pressure me into any long-term commitment.

"Then Alan looked me in the eye and said, 'Tracy, I'd like you to marry me, but only if you're willing to give me a real chance to be loyal to you and to our relationship.' I just started crying and couldn't stop. I cried and cried until I was more drained than I'd ever been. It was as though I were letting out all the anger, fear, resentment, and feelings of betrayal I had refused to let go of all those years since my parents split. If it hadn't been for Alan's gentleness and ability to see through my defense mechanisms, I don't know what may have happened. As it is, we finished college and got married four years ago."

Alan is right. It is vital for adult children of divorce to give others a chance to be loyal to them.

Time and Understanding

Tracy explains, "I've had to learn to give Alan the freedom to be himself and consciously choose to trust him, even when I'm not feeling very much trust inside. Alan gives me the freedom to be myself, too, hang-ups and all. This, in turn, has given our relationship a chance to evolve into a faithful 'belonging' to each other. Alan's favorite saying to me is that I should give him credit for having excellent taste in whom he chooses to love and cherish. He always reminds me that healthy relationships don't crumble into nothingness over disagreements."

Tracy and Alan are very fortunate to be putting together a healthy, interdependent relationship. Tracy's Piggy-Back Child is being nurtured and integrated into her adult personality.

When fear of abandonment and feelings of mistrust and betrayal threaten to overwhelm you, remember:

1. Give the other person a chance to be loyal to you and to your relationship.

2. Let your relationships with family and friends evolve into a faithful "belonging" to each other over a period of time.

3. Give the people in your life credit for seeing your worthiness and having the good sense to place high value on your relationships with them.

4. Remember that functional, healthy relationships do not disintegrate because of arguments, differences, or misunderstanding.

EXERCISE: TRYING PEOPLE THINGS

Sometimes fear of abandonment can permeate your life as a vapor fills a room and you don't even know it. The first key to eliminating fear of abandonment is to recognize it. Read the following scenarios and circle how you would feel if it were you and significant people in your life.

Janet pulled her car to a stop at an intersection and waited for the light to turn green. As she glanced out her window she saw her husband standing with a group of people on the corner, chatting animatedly with a very attractive woman as they waited for the light to change.

1. If this was your spouse and an attractive person of the opposite sex, how would you feel? a. Jealous. b. Angry. c. Curious. d. Betrayed.

Lee and his girlfriend had a date for Saturday evening. Lee's girlfriend is a stewardess for a major airline. Her schedule is sometimes changed unexpectedly. On Saturday when Lee got home there was a message from her on his answering machine: "Hi, hon! Just wanted to let you know that I have a red-eye flight to New York tonight so I have to cancel our date. Talk to you tomorrow night. 'Bye." In the background Lee could hear noises that sounded more like a party than an airport.

2. How would you feel if you were Lee and this was your "significant other"? a. Suspicious. b. Unsettled. c. Disappointed. d. Threatened.

Rita's friend, Marcy, called Rita one evening and told her about having a fabulous lunch with a new friend she had met at work that day. Marcy exclaimed that she couldn't wait for Rita to meet her new friend.

3. How would you feel if you were Rita in this situation? a. Hurt. b. Anxious. c. Indifferent. d. Irritated.

Lori's boss had passed her by for a promotion several months ago, stating that she didn't have enough tenure with the company or experience with the position to promote her this time, but that she would be seriously considered the next time a higher position opened up. Recently, an upper management slot did become available. Lori put in for the promotion. Her boss passed her up again, citing the same reasons.

4. How would you feel if you were Lori? a. Enraged. b. Inadequate. c. Disconcerted. d. Shut out.

Looking at Your Answers

First of all, if you chose any answer other than c—curious, disappointed, indifferent, disconcerted—you most likely suffer with a fear of abandonment.

If you circled more a's—jealous, suspicious, hurt, enraged—there is a strong indication that you have some "partner" problems in your relationships. Extreme jealousy, suspicion, hurt, and rage are often manifestations of a deep fear that a spouse or significant other will abandon you and leave you all alone in the big, bad world.

On the other hand, if most of your answers fell in the b category—angry, unsettled, anxious, inadequate—you show a lot of insecurity. You are afraid of being abandoned and have doubts about your ability to make it on your own.

Finally, mostly d answers—betrayed, threatened, irritated, shut out—imply that your fear of abandonment comes out amid control issues in your life, that you may be constantly on the lookout for and entangled with situations which have to do with controlling people and situations in your life.

Practicing People Things

Fear of abandonment is not a feeling that can be overcome in one five-minute exercise or two short attempts. It may be a deeply rooted fear that was planted in your Piggy-Back Child when your parents divorced or in the aftermath of that happening. But one way you can begin to face and cope with this fear is by "practicing" people things.

For example, if you have problems with jealousy and suspicion you may want to try "letting go" of your spouse or friends by deliberately choosing to believe only good in situations that would otherwise set your mind into overtime detective motion by assuming that your "other" is always preparing to dump you. Choose in your mind to say, "My spouse loves me and will not abandon me." Or, "If this relationship ends I will not be abandoned. I will be okay. But for now, this relationship is fine. I'm fine!"

If your fear of abandonment stems mostly from an overall insecurity, then it is vital that you learn to allow the love, support, and encouragement of other people into your life. Try again to choose to believe the good that other people offer you. Don't let your mind automatically choose to be angry or anxious about real or imagined criticisms, slights, and misunderstandings. Deliberately choose to think well of others.

If the grocery store clerk is grumpy, choose to believe that he is inadvertently expressing some hurt he has recently experienced, which has nothing to do with you, rather than thinking he is rude to you because he does not like you.

If your father criticizes the potato salad you made, choose to believe that he has a right to express his opinion rather than thinking that he hates your cooking.

Finally, if your fear of abandonment makes itself known through frequent feelings of betrayal and irritation with others, then beware of an incessant need to control. It is imperative for you to accept that you cannot control the feelings and actions of others! You cannot force your spouse to stay with you. You cannot make your co-workers like you. You cannot demand that your mother express her love for you in the ways you wish she would.

You must accept that others may abandon you emotionally. And if they do, you have the inner strength to survive. And — you have God. God will not leave you. He will be there regardless of your fears, insecurities, and irrational needs.

Individuals who are operating from a base fear of abandonment often suffer severe problems with low self-esteem. Without a good sense of self-worth it is extremely difficult to have a fulfilling life. Let's look at how the behaviors of others and life's circumstances can affect your self-image.

-7-

Looking at Low Self-Esteem

Margaret and her husband, Howard, divorced when their daughter, Shelly, was eight. Margaret married Jake within a year. Shelly had a crush on Jake from the beginning. Jake, however, remained close to his three children who lived with his first wife, and he was extremely uncomfortable with Shelly's school-girl admiration. He was gruff and unavailable to her. To Shelly this amounted to rejection, and it was a real blow to her ego.

As Shelly grew into pre-puberty and then full-blown adolescence she distanced herself more and more from Jake. The rejected little girl inside did not understand why Jake hugged and loved his biological daughters and son but refused to show affection to her. Shelly's Piggy-Back Child shut off her emotions toward Jake.

Meanwhile, Howard had not been the most consistent father to Shelly. He also remarried after his divorce from

Margaret and moved away for two years. He moved back into town and divorced again. When Shelly was almost twelve, Howard married for the third time. This wife had small children. Shelly visited them on weekends for several months, but her father was totally enamored of his new bride and two darling stepchildren. Shelly, an awkward child on the brink of puberty, was basically relegated to the role of baby-sitter.

By the time she was fourteen, Shelly was terribly insecure and confused. She did not know why she felt so unloved, but she surely did. The natural and normal doubts and hormonal urges of adolescence increased her already confused ego. She did not feel comfortable with Howard and his family, and she and Jake fought bitterly. He refused to accept Shelly as he did his own children, and Shelly retaliated by rejecting anything and everything about Jake.

About this time Howard decided he needed to spend more one-on-one time with Shelly. Shelly, of course, accepted his attention and began to blossom. But soon his third wife began to object to Howard's being away from home on weekends, leaving her with two rambunctious children.

Rejected Again

Howard, torn between two loyalties, soon began to see less and less of Shelly. After several weeks he even quit inviting Shelly to his home. He would call her sporadically and try to talk, but Shelly would not have much to say; she just felt rejected again.

On her sixteenth birthday, Shelly told her mother and Jake that she was spending the night with her girlfriend. When Howard called to wish Shelly happy birthday, Jake gave him the phone number where Shelly could be reached. Howard called back a few minutes later and told Margaret that Shelly was not at her girlfriend's and was not expected.

The next morning, Howard went to Margaret's and Jake's home to wait for Shelly. They watched from the living room window as a teen-age boy pulled up to the curb and Shelly got out of the car.

Shelly did not try to hide what she had done. The boy's parents were out of town and she had spent the night at his house with him. She did not pretend to regret that they had slept together.

Margaret was livid, Jake was disgusted, and Howard was enraged. The three of them got into a battle about who was to blame for Shelly's promiscuous and outrageous behavior. Howard blamed Margaret; Margaret blamed Jake; Jake blamed Howard. They verbally chased one another around until everyone was exhausted. Shelly, listening from her bedroom, was feeling quite pleased that they were all finally paying some attention to her.

Jake suggested sarcastically that if Howard thought he could be a better father maybe Shelly should live with him for awhile. Howard shot back that this was impossible because he and his wife were already separated. Shelly stayed with Margaret and Jake, but the next three years were one long roller coaster ride of turmoil.

Acting Out the Pain

Shelly was soon labeled as "easy" by her school friends. She began to ditch school regularly. Once she ran away and was brought back. She failed some of her courses so she could not graduate with her classmates. She was mouthy and disrespectful.

Margaret and Jake told her she was irresponsible, bratty, dumb, lazy, and useless. As their frustrations mounted, Shelly's negative self-image magnified a hundredfold. Finally, when she turned nineteen, Jake kicked her out of the house, and Margaret stood by him. She had taken all she could of her rebellious daughter's behavior. For Shelly, whose Piggy-Back Child was still trying to find loving acceptance from the people in her life, this was just one more devastating rejection.

Shelly showed up at Howard's doorstep with two suitcases. Reunited with his third wife, Howard was trying to make a go of his marriage, without much success. Beside himself with concern, he felt guilty for his contribution to Shelly's wild and erratic behavior. But he did not want to take responsibility for her. At the same time he saw this as an opportunity to cast blame on Margaret and Jake for Shelly's troubled adolescence.

Howard's wife reluctantly agreed to let Shelly stay for awhile, but the next weeks were a nightmare for all of them. Shelly listened through the arguments Howard and his wife had about her being there, and she fought back when his wife tried to make her help out around the house. Finally, Shelly packed her two suitcases and moved in with a boyfriend. This relationship ended when Shelly came home after work and found her boyfriend in bed with another girl. Completely dejected, Shelly again packed her suitcases and went back to her mother and Jake, begging forgiveness.

What Goes Around Comes Around

By now, Shelly believed everything the significant people in her life had been telling her. She was in fact irresponsible, bratty, dumb, lazy, and useless. She tumbled head first into young adulthood with a self-image that rated zero on the one-to-ten scale.

By the time she was thirty, Shelly had been married and divorced. She had two bright, adorable children by her husband, and an out-of-wedlock infant with whose father she'd had a brief, passionate relationship.

Neither man helped to support the children and her waitress job did not cover all her expenses, even with the help of government food stamps.

One afternoon she got back to her two-bedroom apartment and met the manager with an eviction notice. Shelly panicked. She packed up everything she could carry and loaded kids and belongings into her car and drove to her mother's and Jake's.

By the time Shelly was forty, Jake was dead of a heart attack, Margaret was old and worn out, Howard was again divorced, and Shelly and her three children were living with still another boyfriend. Her own rebellious, moody teenagers had no respect for her. Her boyfriend treated all of them with distaste and they too were feeling the effects of rejection and low self-esteem.

The direction one's self-esteem takes depends on where its roots begin. What parents, grandparents, teachers, and other significant adults say to and about a child impresses upon the child how he/she should feel about himself/herself. A child who is rejected and tossed about emotionally, bounced from person to person and place to place, will get the idea that he is not loved unconditionally by anyone.

When her mother remarried, Shelly went into a new home structure with open arms and a loving heart. Her fragile spirit was bruised by Jake's rejection. Her life took on an abstract momentum that blew her through the years like a leaf in the wind. She never had enough self-esteem to take charge of her own life.

Low self-esteem can cause even the most attractive, intelligent, and talented kids to undermine themselves for their entire lifetimes.

Believing a Lie

When parents divorce, their children's lives are affected in some way forever. The greatest effect is on the children's ego, their self-esteem. The severe adjustment problems many ACDs have can be traced back to the time when their parents divorced or to events following divorce. Some of these problems include alcohol and other drug abuse, physical violence, extremely dysfunctional relationships, paralyzing anxieties, and addictive behaviors of all sorts.

It does not have to be that way, however. Many parents handle their divorce relatively well and manage to keep open lines of communication between themselves, their children, ex-spouses, former in-laws, and new stepfamilies. The little ones in these break-ups may survive to become fairly well-adjusted adults. They may have certain or all the dysfunctions listed here to some extent, but to a much lesser degree than other more unfortunate victims. Many of these adult children of divorce will insist that they were not affected negatively by their parents' divorce in any way. However, some will exhibit symptoms to the contrary, everything from a vague uneasiness in their lives to an obvious need for more love and affection.

These adult children of divorce may have been so conditioned to believe either that their parents' divorce was friendly or necessary (due to life-threatening problems, for example) that they have no "good" reason to be negatively affected by it. They may feel that it would be "disloyal" or "uncalled for" to carry any problems into adulthood that may have resulted from divorce.

This way of thinking on the part of adult children of divorce is directly connected to low self-esteem. These are often ACDs who have been blasted with messages that proclaim, "Your needs are not as important as our needs, so keep them to yourself." Or, "You have it so much better than others that you'd better not dare to complain—you're not worthy of the privilege!" Low self-esteem. The image of self becomes so confused and discouraged that the Piggy-Back Child, snuggled against the heart, becomes broken. He or she believes the lie.

Proving Your Worth

To be able to sleep well at night (and some still don't manage it), most ACDs in this type of self-esteem dilemma grow up with one main mission: gain the approval of others and "prove your own worth." It may not be a conscious mission, but those who have accepted it are all around us. We see it in the man who dotes on his mother; the woman who still behaves flirtatiously as Daddy's little girl; the woman who nearly kills herself to become a doctor when she'd rather be a teacher; the entrepreneur who scales all financial heights before he's thirty but remains lonely and reclusive; the exhibitionist who lives promiscuously; the housewife who never misses cooking a meal and maintains an immaculate house; the man who gives up plans for his life and joins his father's business because he can't properly take care of his own family in his scheme of things; the workaholic whose physician warns him repeatedly to slow down; the couple whose children always have the best bikes, clothes, stereo equipment, and cars.

Yes, nearly everywhere we look we can see the effects of divorce on adult children. We may be able to see these effects, but often ACDs cannot. These people most likely believe the lie that they are not worth much inside, but they certainly put on a great front.

ACD Family "Appendages"

One of the most common ways in which ACD's with low self-esteem subconsciously grapple with proving their worth is via their nuclear or blended families. They seem to shout, "Look, Mom (or Dad)! See me now. I have a nice house, two nice cars, a boat, 2.2 (or 4.8 children), pets, a good job, a college fund for my kids, and wholesome holiday traditions!" It's as though they can erase the blemishes which divorce placed on their lives by providing the "right" lifestyles, educations, or financial portfolios.

And if providing enough does not work, many ACDs resort to living their lives vicariously through their children. In a way their kids become appendages. Reflections of how good or how bad the parents are is revealed by how the kids turn out. It is almost a "pride of ownership." But, as with all deeply planted problem seeds, the tangled roots eventually push a little green sprig of trouble above the ground.

Family Networks That Bind

Jan and Corey have been married twelve years. They have two children, Anna, nine, and Tyler, soon to be six. Jan's parents were divorced when she was eight. Corey is from a nuclear family. However, though legally married, Corey's parents have unfortunately been emotionally divorced for years. Over the years Corey's father has had numerous affairs with other women. After each incidence of infidelity, he begged Corey's mother to stay with him "for the sake of the children." Corey has a lot of sympathy for his mother and feels obligated to her for her sacrifice. On the other hand, he openly disrespects and shuns his father. Corey, thirty-six, has never consciously considered that his mother could have contributed to his father's behavior or been responsible in many ways for the demise of their relationship.

Corey grew up with an image of women as strong, central characters in his life. Inwardly, he believes that he needs Jan in order to survive. His self-esteem is low, and his image of men in general is that they are weaklings camouflaged as macho who cave in to the slightest temptation.

Corey has a subconscious drive to prove that he is not weak, that he is worthy of a woman's respect, and is a good, reliable person who has parlayed these virtues into a remarkably successful lifestyle for his family. With an excellent salary and annual bonuses, he is a member of the upper management team for a large corporation. It is quite common for him to leave work, drive across the city to a baseball game, dance recital, piano audition, or soccer match for one or both of his children. On weekends he keeps up his yard and house, takes his family on various cultural and recreational outings, and makes it a point to take Jan out on regular "dates." For all intents and purposes, Corey is as near to a perfect husband, father, employee, and individual as any upper middle-class suburbanite can be.

Jan is a model wife and mother, an excellent cook and top-flight housekeeper. She is a loan officer at the bank, a PTA Board Member, is on the local Council of Arts and Humanities, and Corey's biggest fan. To onlookers, Jan has it together. She appears to be the woman on commercials who has it all.

But Jan also has low self-esteem. She grew up feeling obligated to a divorced mother who claims she "gave the best years of her life to a lousy husband and pack of selfish, bratty kids." Jan's father thinks he "worked his butt off to pay child support and college tuition and never got one bit of respect in return!" Subconsciously, Jan is driven to prove to her parents that she is not selfish, that she is grateful and is worthy of their love and approval.

Corey and Jan react to their different childhoods in very typical ways. As adults they have not cut the invisible cords that so often bind ACDs (and adult children like Corey of "emotionally divorced parents") to family networks that are stifling and unhealthy, and which foster low self-esteem.

Even though Corey and Jan appear to have a stable marriage and family life, their children are growing up with damage to their self-images because their parents are not conscious that their dysfunctional backgrounds left any negative affects on them.

Nine-year-old Anna wears perfect little outfits to her perfect school, gets perfect marks on her report cards, plays perfect piano at her auditions, and keeps her room perfectly neat.

On the other hand, little brother, Tyler, is a handful. He refuses to conform to the family standards. This is due partly to his birth order, partly to his individual personality, and partly to an instinctive force that puts him on "automatic rebellion" against his parents' attempts to make him into another "perfect little soldier." Of course, Tyler is only six. If Corey and Jan continue their lifestyle patterns of seeking approval and the sense of worth they each so desperately need, Tyler may well give in to the molding process by the time he is Anna's age. Or he may keep on rebelling and grow up to feel inadequate because he could not naturally conform.

Recognizing the Problem

The good news is that recently Corey and Jan attended a seminar on instilling high self-esteem in children. Although they went to get pointers on how to insure that Anna and Tyler grew up to be "as successful" as Corey and Jan, they were both amazed and more than a little unsettled to find that they identified with several of the indicators which described people with low self-esteem.

Driving home in the dark after the seminar, Corey asked Jan, "Would you read me the list of low self-esteem indicators again?"

Jan felt uneasy. There was a real sense of foreboding in the car, as if something bad was going to happen. But she opened the notebook, turned on a little flashlight, and read: "Consider the possibilities that you may have low self-esteem if any of the following apply to you:

"1. You are an adult from a family network that is affected by divorce, abuses, addictions, emotional instability, or other extreme circumstances.

"2. You feel guilty about or incapable of refusing social invitations, requesting appointments at times more convenient for you, turning down requests that you serve on committees, join athletic teams, etc.

"3. You find yourself voicing agreement with other people even if you don't really feel the same way they do.

"4. You avoid confronting people who have mistreated you or taken you for granted.

"5. You tolerate other people interrupting you, making plans for you, or passing their responsibilities on to you.

"6. You think most people are luckier, more successful, or happier than you are.

"7. You feel ashamed of your parents, your upbringing, your brothers and sisters, or other relatives.

"8. You feel uncomfortable or nervous about what others think when they visit your home, meet your spouse and children, or see your automobile for the first time.

"9. You are afraid to disagree with others for fear they will become angry.

"10. You feel guilty when you get angry. You are somewhat ashamed of yourself for getting 'out of control.'

"11. You strive to have your home, personal appearance, children's lives, and career in perfect order at all times.

"12. You feel guilty and anxious spending time doing things you want to do rather than things you think you 'should' be doing.

"13. You frequently say things such as, "'I should be doing . . . , getting . . . , going . . . ,' etc. Or you often make comments such as, 'I'm too fat, plain, uncoordinated,' etc.

"14. You are overly concerned with helping your children be 'the best' in regard to their clothes, grades, positions they play, etc.

"15. You automatically assume your children won't be the best or excel at anything.

"16. You are insecure about contributing any comments to group discussions, reports at work, or community issues that affect you.

"17. You assume that you are doing well to maintain a home, raise children, and keep your job, no matter what dreams you may secretly have for yourself.

"18. You believe you are a failure as a person if you don't provide a certain standard of living for yourself or your loved ones.

"19. You refuse to take any risks to achieve cherished wishes because you feel you would 'probably lose anyway.'

"20. You try to achieve in your life to prove to your parents, family, friends, or stepfamilies that you can."

Jan took a deep breath, shut the notebook, and sat back heavily in her seat. Corey remained silent.

Broken Hearts

Jan and Corey didn't speak the rest of the way home. Their minds were full of troubling thoughts and memories.

Corey drove the sitter home, Jan tucked the kids into bed and climbed under her own covers. As she lay there she remembered a small alabaster vase her mother had given her for her thirteenth birthday. Later that night, after she had gone to bed, she knew for sure that it was too late for her father to call and wish her happy birthday. He had forgotten all about it. She cried hot tears of anger and hurt.

The morning after her birthday, Jan was still so full of rage and disappointment she slammed her hairbrush down on the vanity, nudging the little vase. As if in slow motion she watched helplessly as the pretty alabaster vase wobbled from side to side, toppled off the edge of the vanity, and broke in two pieces on the ceramic tile floor.

Jan felt then as if her heart had cracked with the vase. Tonight, as she waited for Corey to come to bed she felt the way she had on her thirteenth birthday, that her heart was cracking. But she couldn't quite figure out why. Over and over she dreamed about how the alabaster vase fell and broke. Each time it fell she regretted that she had not been able to catch it. She blamed herself for not being quick enough, coordinated enough, or careful enough to retrieve the vase before it hit the floor.

Over the next several days Jan found herself taking the Low Self-Esteem Indicators List from her purse again and again. Each time she looked it over, folded it up, and put it back into her leather bag she felt the same crack in her heart she had felt when the vase hit the bathroom floor.

One afternoon Jan got home early from work. She had planned to take Tyler for a dental appointment, but the dentist's office cancelled due to an emergency. Jan told Tyler to go on to day care after school as he usually did, but she decided to take off work. She made herself a cup of tea. For some reason she felt strange—all quivery inside. The vase incident wasn't the only memory recently that presented itself to her consciousness. She was being flooded with memories from her childhood.

One time, she remembered, shortly after her father had left, he had called her on the phone. Her mother listened in on the extension. When Jan said good-bye and her father had barely hung up, Jan's mother pounced on her. "Next time he fills you full of all that stuff about missing you and loving you, ask him why he left you and why he won't pay a decent amount of child support! Just ask him, Jan. You'll see what kind of a man he really is some day, and then you'll know what I put up with."

Jan remembered another time when her mother and father were screaming obscenities at each other in the driveway. The neighbors on both sides came outside to see what the commotion was about. Jan was so embarrassed she wanted to go back inside. But each time she started to leave, one of her parents would shout, "No! You stay here, little girl. You need to hear just what's going on around here!" Jan had felt like a rubber band about to snap in the middle.

Then there was the time Jan's father took her and her siblings home after a visit to his house. He stomped to the front door, opened it, walked to the middle of the living room floor, and dumped the contents of two suitcases. He shouted to Jan's mother, "There! If you want to complain that I don't do enough for you or the kids, that I don't pay enough support, and I don't help out enough, then I'll give you something to complain about! For your information my wife is sick to death of washing your children's dirty clothes! We've got all we can handle with our kids!"

Jan sighed over her tea as she thought of her stepmother Sal, and her two stepbrothers. The boys had been born only a little over a year apart and they took up most of what was left of her father's attentions to his four "original" children. Sal was less than thrilled on weekends and holidays when her husband's first kids (as she called them) visited. Oh, she had been nice at first. She would bake cookies and plan activities for everyone. But as time went on, Sal seemed to get more and more sour toward Jan and her siblings. She got into arguments on the phone with Jan's mother and eventually discouraged the "first kids" from visiting at all.

Jan thought back to how jealous she had felt when those two little boys got the love and affection from her father that his "first kids" should have gotten. She had hated the boys sometimes, like when her father had forgotten her thirteenth birthday. Then she would feel guilty and ashamed of herself.

The crack in Jan's heart seemed to branch out into other parts of her as more memories came to her. Her tea grew cold in the cup as she got up and looked out the kitchen window. Two teenage girls walked by, giggling and bouncing with energy.

One afternoon when she was fourteen, Jan and her girl-friend bounced along the sidewalk just like these girls. School had let out early and they burst into Jan's house to find her mother in bed with a boyfriend. After that, Jan didn't bring friends home with her unless she knew her mother was out.

Just before Jan turned fifteen, her mother married George. George was a warm, caring man. He treated Jan and the other kids kindly. This made Jan's mother jealous. She accused Jan and her two sisters of flirting with George. She told Jan's brother that he was taking up too much of George's time, begging him to play basketball with him. A few months before Jan turned seventeen, George left her mother. They divorced. The crack in Jan's heart began to splinter into tiny lines of pain.

At her high school graduation, Jan remembered glancing nervously around the auditorium full of people. The school gave students blocks of tickets in the same seating section. Jan wished they had allowed divorced families to split up. She was more anxious about her father, Sal, and the two boys sitting in close proximity to her mother and the "first kids" than she was about the graduation ceremonies.

Jan spotted everyone, sitting with set jaws and stern faces. Jan filed in line to receive her diploma. Instead of feeling proud and confident, she felt worried and insecure. In the courtyard, relatives and friends gathered around the graduates to congratulate them. Jan watched her friends and their loved ones laughing, hugging, and leaving together to celebrate somewhere. Her mother jostled her way through the crowd blaring, "Jan, you will not believe what your father said to that wench he married, right in front of me!"

Hurting to Heal

Standing at the kitchen window, Jan felt the splinters in her heart shatter. Deep aching sobs began somewhere in her stomach. Why!? Why couldn't her family have been normal? Why did her parents have to be divorced? Why did they have to fight and carry on? What was so wrong with her and her sisters and brother that her parents couldn't work it out?

She wasn't selfish! Or was she? She wasn't bratty! Or was she? Back and forth Jan went. Her mental anguish at the thought of what a poor, pathetic person she was overwhelmed her. She thought about how "perfect" she and Corey had tried to make their marriage, children, home life, and careers. She realized that it was all a gigantic smoke screen. They had hidden in the smoke so they would not be able to see how they thought about themselves. She felt anger, guilt, and shame taking over again, just as it had when she was growing up. She thought about sensitive Anna, and how she and Corey had treated her like a little doll to dress up and display. She thought of Tyler and how they had tried to push his boisterous personality into a mold where it did not fit.

Jan began to shout at her parents as if they were in the room. "I hate you! I hate you both for what you did to me! You're the ones who are selfish and horrid! You divorced — we kids didn't! You abandoned us, we didn't leave you! I could never be good enough for you and now I'm trying to make my own children good enough for you! Oh, how I hate you!"

As she screamed out all the agony and despair, even though she was a successful career woman, wife, and mother, Jan wished with all her little girl's shattered heart that her parents had gotten back together and had a "normal" relationship.

She was frightened by the realization that she and Corey, even with all their outward success, carried along with them two anxious Piggy-Back Children. These inner selves were still fighting to prove that their haunted pasts and they as people meant something. Even as Jan allowed herself to hurt so deeply, she was allowing herself to begin to heal.

MANAGEMENT: GETTING A POSITIVE SELF-IMAGE

Fortunately, Corey had been having his own experiences with insight and awareness. He had realized that even though his parents were still technically married, they might just as well have been divorced, and that his was a dysfunctional family network in a different way than Jan's. Corey also kept thinking about the Self-Esteem Seminar and had been working through his own share of anger, guilt, and shame. He recalled many incidents during his growing up which demanded his attention now and prompted him to see that in reality he had a very poor self-image.

That evening, when Corey got home from work, Anna and Tyler were in front of the television set alone. Corey knew immediately that something was wrong because he and Jan never let the kids watch programs unsupervised. He greeted the kids with his usual dutiful kiss to the tops of their heads and went looking for Jan.

He found her in their bedroom, curled up tightly hugging a pillow, sobbing her heart out. Corey quickly went to her and pleaded with her to tell him what was wrong. Jan clung to Corey and gulped out enough for him to know what had triggered the hysteria. That night, for the first time ever, Anna and Tyler were allowed to eat delivered-in pizza in front of the TV. They were also allowed to go to bed without a bath, which was nearly unheard of in their household.

Jan and Corey stayed up most of the night sharing their painful memories and the anguish they felt over their lost childhoods. They both called in sick the next morning, something neither of them had ever done before without really having a medical illness. They spent the whole day together. They cried and laughed together, and decided that they would, with each other's help, build a new life for themselves and their children, one where they really liked who they were and could honestly say they thought highly of themselves. They were going to get positive self-images!

Corey and Jan wisely consulted a professional counselor who guided them in their search for ways to integrate their hurting Piggy-Back Children with their newly aware adult selves.

One of the first things each of them did after their initial visit to the counselor was to list the major areas of their lives and to list separate needs within each area. This was extremely difficult because they had lived outside their own unique personalities nearly all their lives. They did not know what they wanted in the beginning, but as they practiced over several weeks a clearer picture of who they were and what was really important to them began to emerge (see Figure 2).

Each night, after Anna and Taylor were asleep, Corey and Jan took out their Master List and brainstormed different ways to meet their needs. They talked about life changes, everything from jobs to frequency of contact with family and friends. They talked about moving, starting to attend church, and putting the kids in a private school. It was a very pleasureable adventure for them as they played with ideas that were just for them and not designed to fulfill the expectations of others.

It was enjoyable to consider anything and everything a possibility.

Master List of Areas of Life and Needs		
Need	Corey	Jan
Self (person)	more peaceful lifestyle	quieter, less hectic pace
Marriage	more alone time with wife	more relaxed time together
Parenthood	fewer structured activities	more one-on-one time with kids
Self (career)	Less demanding job	my own business
Extended Family	less to do with my parents & siblings	let go of old pain— more relaxed relationships
Friends	seek out supportive friendships	nurture present friendships
Community	drop my roles on boards, committees, etc.	keep active role
Spiritual	renew relationship with God	find a relationship with God
Other		

Figure 2

It was a wonderful awakening to begin to take care of themselves.

It was delightful to validate their own feelings, needs, and expectations rather than negate them.

It felt good to begin to believe that they were worthy of love and attention unconditionally.

It was challenging to take the time to figure out what they really wanted from life.

Additionally, it was very rewarding to make a conscious plan to fulfill their own needs.

Finally, it was exciting to implement their plan.

Corey and Jan worked with their therapist on a weekly basis to discover and bring many painful emotions into the open through discussing, remembering, examining, and experiencing the feelings. They learned to let go of the heartbreak of issues that had haunted them since childhood and to which they had clung doggedly into adulthood like Piggy-Back Children.

The therapist helped them to understand that most parents do not intentionally hurt their children or squelch their self-esteem. He led them to see that parents do the best they can at the time, and it is not the job of adult children to heal or take care of their parents.

Jan was able to begin to put her past into perspective by pretending that her parents and significant others in her life were in the room with her. She told them exactly how she felt about them and the growing up she had experienced. She consciously chose to let go of the hurt and suffering she had experienced at the hands of the self-focused adults in her life. It was very difficult and she could not honestly say that she had forgiven them, but she managed to put her life into a forward motion.

Corey, on the other hand, found it necessary to confront his parents with his feelings. He went to their home by himself and bravely told them how their lives had affected him. He expressed his feelings of inordinate obligation on to his mother, the resentment and repulsion he felt for his father, and the bitterness he had toward them for discounting him as a child. When it was all over, Corey's parents were very angry at and hurt by their son. They said he was just trying to push the blame for his problems off on them and they would have none of it! Corey parted with hostile words exchanged among the three of them and went home full of remorse and self-hatred.

However, as time went on, Corey began to feel better for taking the initiative to validate his emotions by putting them into words and confronting his parents. His guilt began to subside as he grew healthier. One day he was able to call them and tell them he was sorry that they felt badly; but he reminded them that what he said was true and he hoped they could have a friendly relationship in the future.

Although Corey's parents would not give an inch, Corey had done what he could to honor himself and them. He could then proceed to live within his own skin; he was integrating his Piggy-Back Child into his adult personality.

Jan, even though she could not bring herself to forgive her parents for all the things they had done or exposed her to, was also integrating her personality by accepting where she was at the moment and that it was all right to be there.

In fact, Jan was extremely grateful to her therapist for pointing out Mark 12:30 and 31, "'Love the Lord your God with all your heart and with all your soul and with all your mind and with all your strength. . . . 'Love your neighbor as yourself.' There is no commandment greater than these."

In discussing these verses, Jan decided that if she learned to love herself—faults and all—then she could love the people who had hurt her without saying that what they had done was okay. In this way, Jan's hostility and guilt were greatly diminished. For now, total forgiveness could be God's department. Jan sincerely believed that love was the key; forgiveness could take time to happen.

In fact, 1 Peter 4:8 says exactly that: "Above all, love each other deeply, because love covers over a multitude of sins."

Jan had never had any religious instruction or held any particular beliefs in God. But she yearned for a relationship with God that was bigger than the everyday realities of life. She immediately drew close to the idea of a God who loved her regardless of her flaws or weaknesses.

She was especially helped by the security of knowing that while God loved her for just exactly who she was. He wanted her to be a whole, loving person. He also would do the same and wanted the same for her parents and others. This gave Jan great comfort because it removed the responsibility of her parents from her shoulders; her business was between her and God, and so was theirs.

Instinctively, Jan sensed that God would not want her to heal herself by ripping her parents apart—loving herself at the expense of their being human. So she let them be and got on with her own life. The release was tremendous.

Taking the Weight off Your Shoulders

As Corey and Jan learned to accept each of their own pasts, they were able to begin to accept themselves as human beings of value to their own selves, each other, their children, their employers, their extended families, friends, and to God. They realized that people are not hooked together permanently as appendages. They saw that just because a hand moved did not mean a foot had to move also. They knew that because a parent hurts, a child does not have to suffer permanent damage. When a parent moves, a child does not necessarily have to move also.

Corey and Jan now understood that no one is so bad, fat, ugly, lazy, poor, stupid, useless, or unsuccessful that he or she can cause a parent to get divorced or children to grow up to be failures. Adult children must come to a place where they put their pasts to rest and become fully accountable for the quality of their lives.

This is by no means to say that gaining a good sense of self-esteem is an easy task. It can be grindingly difficult where there is complicated destruction done to a child's psyche—when a child has been sexually molested, for example, by a parent, stepparent, step-sibling, a parent's boyfriend or girlfriend, or there has been physical violence, emotional abuse, or other extremely painful circumstances in his or her life. Then, professional help is strongly advised to help work through problems.

When it comes to mending broken hearts, there are no

"garden-variety" problems or "quick-grow" solutions. ACDs must grant themselves the necessary time and effort to learn to love themselves. Taking care of self is not a luxury, it is an inherent right of being human.

The steps that Corey and Jan followed toward gaining a better self-image and developing good self-esteem may be of help to you too:

1. Realize that you cannot live to fulfill the expectations of others.
2. Consider anything and everything you have ever dreamed of as a possibility.
3. Begin to love and take care of yourself.
4. Accept that your feelings, needs, and expectations are valid.
5. Believe you are worthy of unconditional love and attention.
6. Take the time and make the effort to think through what you want for your life.
7. Make a plan to fulfill your needs.
8. Implement that plan and make it work for you!

Regardless of whether you find it necessary to confront your parents or others (as Corey did), or choose to put things into perspective by imagining that you are speaking your feelings aloud to those who have brought destruction into your life (as Jan did), it is vital for you allow to yourself time to become aware, think through, cope with the pain, and let go of the past.

There are no pat answers and every adult child of divorce deals with his/her scars in his/her own unique way and time schedule.

For now, let God take care of the business of loving and forgiving those who have hurt you. Concentrate on your own relationship with God and let Him love you. Remember, He does not want you to build up your own self-esteem at the expense of another person's life. He loves everyone exactly as they are at the moment.

Accept that every person has intrinsic value and worth; nobody is totally unlovable. And every adult must be accountable for the quality of his own life. You cannot cause another person's demise.

It can be very difficult to take good care of yourself, especially if you have grown accustomed to negating your feelings, needs, and expectations. Practice the following exercise.

Exercise: Trying People Things

It is easy for other people to tell you to take good care of yourself, isn't it? They are not the ones who have to live in your shoes and meet all the demands you have to live with. They don't have to answer your phone, pay your bills, debate spouse, or solve the other problems you may have at home or work.

When you live with low self-esteem the normal, everyday problems of life can magnify themselves a hundred times over. Low self-esteem does not mean a day here and there where you feel like your stomach's pouchy, you look funny with a balding head, or your hips are too wide. Low self-esteem means that you don't think highly enough of yourself to take good care of you. Low self-esteem means that you usually put the needs of others ahead of your own, and to do what's healthy and best for you is the exception to the rule.

Partially you do what's loving toward yourself when you have high self-esteem; but partially you get high self-esteem by doing what is loving toward yourself.

Try the following daily regimen for one month and see if you begin to feel better about who you are. It doesn't matter what names you were called as a youngster, how many times your divorcing parents put you in the middle, or even if your stepmother hated you. You can still get higher self-esteem because you are valuable just the way you are today and just the way you may be next year.

Take a piece of paper, a chalkboard, or anything else you write on and hang it up in a highly visible place. Down the left side write the following list. Put the numbers across the top.

	1	2	3	4	5	6	7	8	9	10	11	12	13	14	15	16	17	18	19	20	21	22	23	24	25	26	27	28	29	30
Eat something healthy for breakfast																														
Call or visit one person you think highly of																														
Do one unpleasant task you'd rather put off																														
Eat something nutritious for lunch																														
Do one-half hour of exercises																														
Do one nice thing for yourself																														
Do one nice thing for someone else																														
Smile at yourself in the mirror and say, " I am a loveable person!"																														
Eat a well balanced dinner																														
Do one thing especially relaxing for you																														
Get in bed one-half hour early and listen to music you enjoy																														
Say, "Thank You Lord, for loving me just the way I am!"																														

Figure 3

(See Figure 3.)

Each day put a check under the date as you complete your list. You may need consciously to create what you are doing at first, but it will become more automatic with time. For example, in the beginning you may think, *Who should I call? What have I been putting off? What's something nice to do for me, for someone else? And what's relaxing?*

Soon you may find yourself enthusiastically saying, "Aah! I'm going to call Aunt Liza today. I'm going to drop the clothes at the dry cleaners today. I'm going to rest in the sun or shade a half hour at lunch. I'm going to send a card to Beth, and I'll relax while I garden."

Caring for yourself doesn't always come automatically, even if you do have a high self-esteem; but it happens more often than not. If you have a low self-image it's extremely important that you start to take good care of yourself most of the time.

Sometimes the Piggy-Back Child that interferes with developing good self-esteem is called loneliness. Loneliness can be a terrific burden — even for those whose lives teem with other people and activities. We'll look at that in the next chapter.

-8-

Loneliness Is Not Just Being Alone

Loneliness is not the same as being alone! Our culture often portrays individuals on their own as being lonely. Commercials, television shows, and many media stories show lone teens who are suicidal, young adults using "Dial-A-Party" lines as they sit alone in their apartments, middle-aged adults hitting the bottom on alcohol and other drug abuse, and the elderly or handicapped sitting in wheelchairs off in some corner of a room. The implication is that these people are lonely. They may very well be, but it's not necessarily because they're alone.

The simple fact is that often, many people who are literally surrounded by others daily are among the most painfully lonely. The loneliest people can be found in crowds. Some dread holidays and other "people" occasions and feel condemned to "watch life pass them by."

Some people fear their uniqueness—and some fear their similarity to others. Adult children of divorce are particularly

151

vulnerable to both ends of this spectrum. On the one side they are anxious about being "different" from what they may consider "normal" members of nuclear families. On the other, they commonly wince at being lumped into the same category as other family members of divorce. The truth is they are each different and each the same. No matter where we're from, what our backgrounds are, or what lifestyle we enjoy, we each have unique characteristics. And we are all the same when it comes to our human needs. When anyone suffers, it just plain hurts.

Likewise, loneliness is loneliness—whether we are ten years of age or fifty, live on an Iowa farm, or in a Manhattan penthouse, or have a family of one or a dozen.

There are those people who thoroughly enjoy their own company. And there are those whose walls seem to close in and suffocate them when they're alone. Those who suffer with actual loneliness know it is not a happy state.

Feeling Cheated Out of Happiness

It is easy to see that adult children of divorce, struggling with such things as dysfunctional relationships, frantic lives, insecurities, fears, or loneliness, may feel cheated out of happiness. It is fairly easy to understand why.

Although this book is in no way meant to be a criticism of parents who divorce, it is vital to be realistic about the many potentially devastating effects that divorce does have on children. As we have seen, the effects can follow many children into adulthood. And until ACDs can come to a place of knowledge, wisdom, and understanding about themselves and their lives, there can be little progress toward freedom from the Piggy-Back Children that hang around their necks—still reacting from the childhood, emotional places where they were wounded and hurt by what was happening to and around them.

It is essential to get to a frame of mind where the ACD can look back upon his or her parents' divorce and the years following and say, "That was then, this is now, and I can become a better person because of it!"

Second Corinthians 5:17 says, "Therefore, if anyone is in Christ, he is a new creation; the old has gone, the new has come!" Until there is a new beginning, after an ACD has put his past to rest emotionally, physically, mentally, and spiritually, there can be a feeling that he has been cheated out of happiness because of the way his parents handled their own life decisions and the lives of their children.

If an adult child of divorce feels cheated out of happiness in life, it is understandable why she could also suffer from extreme loneliness. Liz feels as if she has been lonely ever since her dad left home when she was five. She loved her dad, adored him in fact, and she missed him terribly when he left home. Liz never heard from her dad again.

Actually, 30 percent of all fathers who leave home because of divorce never come back.[1] Understandably, their children quite often become adults with a real fear of abandonment. Many of them also feel cheated out of happiness, and they are lonely.

Liz, for example, is now thirty-two. She grew up with her bitter, contentious mother who remarried and divorced twice after Liz's dad left. Liz's second stepfather was around when Liz was a pretty teenager. He hardly paid any attention to Liz until the newness of his marriage to her mother began to wear off. Then he began to focus more and more of his affections toward Liz. This terrified her.

Yet, if he was going to stick around and it would keep her mother happy, what was a hug or a pat on the behind once in a while? One night, however, he came to Liz in her bedroom and made an unmistakable effort to seduce her into having sexual relations with him.

Liz was repulsed and frightened to the core. She wiggled out of the man's embrace and told him to leave immediately or she would tell her mother. He shot back that if she did, he'd tell her mother how Liz had been "asking for it." Thankfully, he did leave her alone then. Liz fretted all night over what to do. She wasn't in second grade any more. If she had been she could have followed her teacher's instructions to go immediately to her mother and say she'd been touched in places that made her uncomfortable.

This was a whole different situation and time of life. If she told her mother, Liz could see only one of two things happening—either her mother would cause an ugly scene and send her miserable husband packing, or she wouldn't believe Liz, and who knew what repercussions there would be then? Neither reaction would be good for Liz because her mother's bitterness was hard enough to live with now. It would be unbearable if a third husband hit the road!

In the end, Liz didn't say anything to anyone. She was ashamed that this had happened at all and wondered if maybe she had done something to encourage her stepfather's advances. For weeks Liz lived in lonely depression. As life buzzed on around her, she felt as if she were in a glass cage watching it go by.

Then her stepfather left home for other reasons—he said because he couldn't tolerate her mother's complaining and harping anymore. Liz was relieved at his departure, but she was left hopelessly entangled with her bitter, miserable mother.

As a child Liz had fantasies that her biological father would reappear on the doorstep one day, sweep her mother away with loving apologies, and the three of them would live happily ever after. That was the fantasy.

In reality, Liz thought she and her mother were probably the only ones in the world who weren't happy. Even her classmates, whose parents were also divorced, discussed their fantasies of their parents' reconciliation—except Liz thought their fantasies were more valid than hers because most of them had some kind of relationship with their fathers. Liz felt completely cheated out of the happiness she was sure everyone else had.

Isolation Keeps Loneliness Alive

The last two years of high school Liz withdrew more and more. She attended classes, went to her part-time job at a local pizzeria, did her homework, listened to her mother complain to friends on the phone or over coffee, and then slept restlessly until it was time to get up and do it all over again.

Liz's mother was so full of resentment for the way her own life was that she didn't really notice when Liz stopped asking to go out on Friday nights or to have a few girlfriends over on Saturday.

Liz isolated herself. She slipped farther and farther into the grasp of loneliness and despair. By her senior year of high school she truly believed that nobody was ever really happy — that life was one long string of disappointments and problems.

She refused invitations from her friends at school, her co-workers, and perceptive adults who tried to pull her back into the mainstream of life. Nothing worked. Liz became as full of bitterness, resentment, and anger at her "lot in life" as her mother was.

Liz's fantasies of her family's reunion turned into wakeful dreams of finding her father and venting her rage on him with all kinds of unspeakable verbal and physical venom. She also had daydreams of what she'd tell her mother if she dared — all the rotten things Liz had suffered because of two irresponsible parents.

Liz became obsessed with her resentment. She blamed her parents for every single unpleasant thing in her life. She blamed her parents for her loneliness, isolation, hopelessness, resentment, bitter attitude, the advances of her stepfather, not having friends, and even for the blemishes she had on her face.

Now, as Liz approaches middle age, she has immersed herself in a deep pool of loneliness and despair. She only "comes up for air" when it is absolutely necessary — when she must get her groceries, go to the bank, or mail a letter. Without intensive professional help it is unlikely that Liz will change much. She'll probably be miserable the rest of her life.

Loneliness Stays with Misery

The saying goes, "Misery loves company." Yes, and the company is loneliness. Have you ever noticed that the most miserable people you know are often those who frantically go to coffee at one friend's house then another's, show up at company picnics, school functions, board meetings, and social occasions armed with their grandest complaints and tales of woe?

We all have our moments of misery, but if they are so frequent that we are constantly bombarding others with them, chances are we are really very lonely inside.

People need people. We are inherently social creatures. Although some of us are more reclusive or introverted than others, we still cannot survive as whole human beings without connecting ourselves to others.

Adult children of divorce are particularly vulnerable to loneliness because their ideas of how people connect, communicate, love, interdepend, and treat one another has often been so damaged that they become frightened and jaded when involved in relationships with others—and themselves.

Vicki was six when her parents, Deb and Kurt Thompson, separated. They were extremely civilized about the whole thing and determined to split everything in half—including child custody. Since both parents resided within the boundaries of the same school district, it was decided that Vicki would spend one week with her mother and one week with her father. However, her younger brother, Adam, was only two and he would stay with Deb except for weekend visits until he was five. They alternated like this, with few interruptions, for three years until Vicki's fourth grade teacher, Mrs. Lewis, who was very bold and outspoken, called both Vicki's parents into school for a conference.

Mrs. Lewis made no pretenses as to what the situation was in her mind. "Mr. Thompson," she looked from Kurt to Deb, "Mrs. Thompson, I am extremely concerned about Vicki's well-being and I think it's vital that we have honest communication about it."

Kurt and Deb asked that Mrs. Lewis please call them by their first names and indicated they were ready for her to proceed.

Mrs. Lewis did so without hesitation. "I've watched Vicki since she came to this school in kindergarten. She was a bright, outgoing little girl. I have seen her change extensively since your divorce. While I admire your attempt to equitably share custody of your children, I must tell you that in my opinion you are destroying your child."

Kurt leaned forward in his chair, "Now wait one minute, Mrs. Lewis!"

"No, Kurt," Mrs. Lewis quickly stopped him, "I know you love Vicki and I think you would be wise to hear me out — even if it is painful."

Mrs. Lewis hurried on before Kurt could balk, "Vicki has become a withdrawn, exhausted, and lonely child. She bounces from one house to the next, week after week. Some mornings she comes to school with breakfast, some without. Some mornings she's clean and neat, others she's unkempt and frazzled.

"We've had a meeting here at school and we've decided to approach you about this because Vicki is quickly falling behind in her school work. She's been absent with illness an excessive number of days, and we see her isolating herself on the playground more and more."

Deb's heart thumped wildly in her chest and she felt flushed all over. What were they doing to their daughter? She asked quietly, "What would you suggest we do to help Vicki?"

"I'm not a family counselor," Mrs. Lewis stated. "I won't pretend to have the answers, but I strongly suggest group therapy and possibly individual counseling for Vicki as well."

Kurt would not let go of his initial defensiveness. He put his hands down on the edge of Mrs. Lewis' desk hard and looked across it right into her eyes as he said, "I will say this — I appreciate your concern for my daughter, Mrs. Lewis. But no one, and I *mean n*o one, will tell me how to take care of her!"

Mrs. Lewis was not ruffled in the least, "I am not telling you how to take care of her. What I am telling you is this: Her behavior shows dramatically that whatever changes have been made at home in recent years are, in fact, negatively affecting her personality and ability to interact with others. You'll have to take things in hand between you and your ex-wife from here."

"Oh, I'll take things in hand, all right!" Kurt almost shouted. "I'll take Vicki out of this school and put her in another one where the parents are respected!"

"I wouldn't do that." Mrs. Lewis' voice was even and sure. "It would be another devastating blow to Vicki's ego."

Deb was shaking all over. Involuntarily, memories of her own parents' divorce when she was Vicki's age tumbled around in her mind. The fear, the nightmares, the daydreams of their getting back together, the dread of their arguments with her and her siblings in the middle, the tears, the anger, guilt, shame, and the awful loneliness all came back to her.

Deb sat paralyzed. She was completely powerless to fight Kurt for Vicki's well-being. She didn't know how. She'd been powerless at nine and now, more than twenty years later, she still felt powerless.

Kurt bellowed at Mrs. Lewis, "I'll be the judge of what's devastating to my own child! Deb, let's go—this woman has taken enough of our time!"

Deb looked helplessly at Mrs. Lewis. She wanted to stay and ask many more questions about Vicki's behavior and how to get help. But, as if computerized to act against her will, she gave a quick nod of her head to Mrs. Lewis and followed Kurt to the hall.

Accountability Can Be Painful

With sorrow in her heart, Mrs. Lewis watched them leave. She wisely knew that behind Kurt's anger was a lonely, insecure, and frightened little boy. The thought that he could hurt his own child because of his life choices was so unbearably painful that he denied the possibility altogether.

Deb, on the other hand, wanted to open up. She wanted to do what was best for Vicki. Mrs. Lewis was sure of this. She could see it in Deb's eyes as the younger woman obediently followed her ex-husband out of the room.

In the years following the huge divorce exodus of couples from traditional marriage and family networks, Mrs. Lewis had seen variations of the same scenario dozens of times. She knew it was silly to think that any major departure from the cultural norm would not also require major adjustments and painful self-examination. After all, more than a million children each year go through their parents' divorces.[2] Considering all the couples, children, extended family members, friends, and other loved ones involved, the implications were staggering!

In Mrs. Lewis's eyes, there was no question about who should be top priority in the aftermath of divorce — the children. But too often the divorcing couple was so focused on their own needs that the children were forced to live on bits and pieces of the love and attention they had received before their parents split up.

Deb knew this for certain — she'd been through it. As she and Kurt reached the parking lot and headed for their separate cars, she wanted to strike out at Kurt. She wanted to scream at him. She wanted to tell him how wrong he was — that Vicki needed their understanding and help. Deb wanted to make him realize that, even though all divorces happened under the unique circumstances of the couples involved, the pain was the same for every child of divorce! She wanted to lay him out flat for using his power and domineering ways to manipulate her and the children — even three *years* after the divorce!

But Deb didn't express any of this aloud to Kurt. She just gave him a helpless wave and said she'd drop Vicki off in two days for her week with Kurt. As Deb drove her car onto the street, she hated herself for her inability to assert what she knew was true. She ached with the lonely helplessness that felt like a living thing inside her.

Deb had been so certain that the joint custody arrangement was the right thing for her children. She thought it would alleviate the longing for the parent who left home. Even as an adult, Deb still felt the loneliness of missing her mom after her parents' divorce. Deb's mom had run away with another man. And Deb could hear her dad bad-mouthing and brainwashing Deb and her siblings about their mom as clearly in her mind today as she could two decades before. Deb had wanted to avoid such excruciating pain for Vicki and Adam no matter what.

But the joint custody arrangement wasn't helping. It was hurting! What should she do? Deb was too intimidated by Kurt to communicate openly with him. She couldn't bring herself to stand up to him. The rest of the day and throughout the night, she fretted and fumed. She resolved to "save" her children. And she had two days to do it.

Doing Wrong for Right Reasons

The next morning Deb called the school and told them Vicki and Adam were ill. She told the kids they were going on a short vacation. The night before she had packed and loaded their suitcases into her car. She trembled as she locked the front door. But she would save her children.

In Deb's eyes, to save her kids meant getting them away from the erratic schedule she and Kurt had imposed on them. She drove to the bank and withdrew all her money so Kurt couldn't track her down if she made future withdrawals from a different location. Deb had thought of everything—even that it was feasible for her to face a jail sentence if she were caught kidnaping her children. But Deb didn't care anymore. She'd sat paralyzed long enough. This was a heroic act of mobilization to Deb. She justified doing wrong because she thought it was for the right reasons.

However, Deb wasn't being accountable to herself—she wasn't facing and coping with her own loneliness, inadequacies, and despair. She was trying to escape them.

Deb and the two children drove all day and well into the night. They stopped to eat quick meals, get gas, and use restrooms. Deb wasn't exactly sure where she was going, but she figured in two days she could get to a decent-sized city several states away before Kurt would start looking for the kids. Deb would call him, tell him she'd moved and why. She wouldn't tell him where, though, because he'd come after them.

The second night, Deb and the kids were near Dallas, Texas. Deb checked them into a motel. It was getting late. Kurt would be worried by now. Her hands were shaking as she dialed the number. Kurt answered his phone after only half a ring.

Deb felt an overpowering lump rise in her throat. She choked out, "Kurt—It's Deb. I—uh—Kurt. Vicki wants to talk to you."

Deb covered the mouthpiece. She could hear Kurt hollering her name and demanding to know what was wrong. She pushed the phone toward nine-year-old Vicki and instructed, "Tell your daddy we've moved. But don't tell him where we are. Just tell him you're okay and I'll call him in a few days."

Vicki took the phone. Her wide eyes were frightened and confused. She said, "Hi, Daddy. It's Vicki."

Kurt blasted Vicki with questions, "Vicki! Are you all right? Where are you? What has your mother done with you? Where's Adam? Is he all right?"

Vicki's voice was nearly a whisper, "Yes, Daddy, we're all right. We moved with Mommy. Mommy said she'll call you in a few days."

Deb stared sternly at Vicki and held her hand out for the phone. Vicki gulped, "Bye, Daddy!" and let the receiver drop to the table. Vicki had never seen her mother like this.

Adam cried in the background that he wanted to talk to his daddy. Deb could hear Kurt screaming as she hung up the phone. She told the kids to get their pajamas on and get into bed. When they were under the covers, she sat near them on the edge of the bed.

Deb simply said, "Don't worry, everything will be okay. We're going to start a new life here where you two can live at one house all the time and not be so tired anymore."

The children were terrified. Whatever was going on they knew it was bad. First, their parents got one divorce and now it seemed they were going to get another.

In the next few days Deb rented a furnished apartment, bought minimum necessities at a large discount store to run a household, registered the kids at a new school, and searched the classifieds for job possibilities.

It was nearly a week later before she had enough courage to call Kurt again. She waited until the children were in bed and then dialed his number. He answered immediately. His voice was full of worry, "Deb! Deb, don't hang up now. We'll work this out. Please talk to me!"

Deb felt deep compassion for Kurt, but she'd heard, "We'll work this out," one too many times to believe it. This really meant, "I'll get my way, Deb, so just listen and do what I say!" She waited silently for Kurt's usual tirade of instructions and criticisms to begin.

Nothing happened except a series of clicking noises on the phone. Then Deb heard Kurt's whimper, "Please, honey, please tell me what's going on. Why did you take the kids?"

Deb felt the lump threaten in her throat again. But she pushed on, "Because, Kurt, Mrs. Lewis was right, we're killing Vicki and we'll kill Adam too if we pull them back and forth like this anymore.

"The kids need stability and we need counseling. I'm going to make sure we have both! These kids aren't going to grow up as I did — all crazy inside because their parents couldn't see past the ends of their noses to help them!"

Kurt pleaded with Deb, "Please, please bring them back! We'll change things. We'll all go to counseling!"

Deb was suddenly filled with rage, "No!" she cried. "You're just like my dad, Kurt! You'll lie, cheat and steal to get your own way — what's best for you — and to get back at me! You're not really thinking about the kids at all! I'm in the driver's seat now, Kurt! You left me, remember? I didn't want the divorce — you did! Now you have to pay for your choice!"

The tone of Kurt's voice changed abruptly from begging to sarcasm. "We'll see about that, Deb, we'll see."

He hung up. Deb felt panic prickle at the back of her neck. Kurt knew something she didn't. She just wouldn't call him again.

She didn't need to call Kurt. She found out what Kurt was up to several days later. As she was preparing dinner, a knock came at the door. Thinking it was a pesky salesman, Deb wasn't surprised to see a nicely dressed gentleman when she opened the door. However, the gentleman signaled over his shoulder and two other men in suits got out of a large sedan in the parking lot. Panic prickled at Deb's neck again.

"Who are you?" she demanded to know. "What do you want?"

The first man simply smiled and drawled, "Ma'am, my name is Roger. I'm here to get your children for their father."

Deb tried to slam the door shut. But within ten minutes the three men had stuffed the children's clothes into plastic garbage bags and left with Vicki and Adam screaming in their arms.

Deb sat in the middle of the living room floor. She had never felt so crushed, lonesome, abandoned, and miserable in her life.

Paying a High Price for a Choice

Deb knew instinctively that she had sacrificed more than what she could bear—her actions would cost her the children. As if in a trance, she packed up what meager belongings were left in the apartment and loaded the car. In the morning she called the school, contacted the complex manager, disconnected her utilities, and left.

When she arrived back at her home two days later there was a message from her attorney on the answering machine, "Deb, it is extremely urgent that you call me." There was also a message from Vicki and Adam. They each said they were going to stay at their daddy's for awhile. Deb's heart broke into a thousand pieces. She sobbed herself to sleep that night. And she visited her attorney the next day with a chilling fear that consumed her body.

Over the next several months there were court hearings, papers served, depositions taken, professional testimonies given, and social workers' recommendations offered. The children stayed with Kurt. Deb was allowed supervised visitation rights by court order. She had to meet Kurt and the kids at neutral, public places and spend time with Vicki and Adam while Kurt observed from a distance.

In the end, Kurt was awarded permanent custody of the children and Deb was to follow strict guidelines in order to have the children with her at home on Saturdays and holidays from 8:00 a.m. to 8:00 p.m.

The loneliness that invaded every nook and cranny of Deb's life was so painful she needed tranquilizers to get through the days and sleeping pills to survive the nights.

Vicki withdrew into herself completely. Adam seemed to be adjusting extremely well to the turmoil he'd been through — until his puppy died.

Kurt called Deb one afternoon. The concern in his voice was genuine as he spoke, "Deb, Adam's puppy got run over in the street this morning. He is hysterical. He's crying for you. Could you come over?"

Deb hurried right over to Kurt's. Adam was curled into a little pile on top of his bed; his shoulders heaved in emotional exhaustion. When Deb laid a hand on his shoulder he hopped into her arms and would not let go.

Vicki stood in the doorway for a long while. She watched her mother cradle Adam and Adam cling to Deb. Inside, Vicki felt a tiny spark of hope. Her father had really needed help with Adam. Maybe her parents would get back together now and things would be all right.

Eventually Adam fell into a listless sleep. Deb lay on the bed beside him and slept the first natural sleep she'd had in months. But both Deb and Adam awoke from their temporary refuge emotionally drained and confused.

Over the next several days Adam's grief over the loss of his puppy grew out of what seemed to be all proportion. Much of the time he was despondent and sullen. Otherwise, he was crying or angry. Kurt was beside himself. Adam would not let Deb out of his sight. Deb was sleeping on Kurt's sofa. Kurt's girlfriend wasn't happy with this arrangement at all. Finally, out of desperation, Kurt suggested they take Adam to a psychologist.

Dr. Evans quickly assessed the problem. He told Kurt and Deb that Adam was exhibiting symptoms of reacting to what professionals termed the "Sleeper Effect." This is an outpouring of the pain and suffering experienced during the traumas of divorce, but repressed at the time. Some children do not give vent to their anguish until they suffer another loss—then they react to this loss with an intensity that seems exaggerated to the loss.[3]

This was what had happened to Adam. He'd lost his parents as a couple. Then he'd lost his father temporarily when Deb abducted the children. Then he lost his mother's regular attentions in the custody battle. Losing his puppy (who had been the answer to the inconsistencies and loneliness in his life) was the last straw.

Kurt consented to a few weeks of group counseling. But as soon as Adam seemed to feel his old self again Kurt called a halt to the sessions. The psychologist advised against this. Deb begged Kurt to keep going. Kurt would have none of it, insisting that he could take care of his own.

The broken family unit limped along over the years. As Vicki's thirteenth birthday approached she decided she didn't want to go to her mother's on Saturdays any more. In fact, she didn't want to see her mother at all. She was fed up with all the bad-mouthing, lying, spying, and tit-for-tat games she'd been forced to play, sandwiched between her parents all these years.

By the time Vicki turned eighteen, she'd been escaping her pain and loneliness with drugs and alcohol for four years! Her parents didn't even know it. The chaos of their childhood took its toll on Adam as well. He was fourteen when Vicki graduated from high school. Like his sister, he'd withdrawn from the mainstream. His grief and loneliness after Vicki left home for college drove Adam to alcohol and drug abuse the same as his sister. Adam went off to college as an irritable, anxious young adult.

Kurt had remarried when his children were twelve and eight. Deb had remarried when they were sixteen and twelve. The two separate couples did not have the time, energy, or focus their children needed for healthy guidance. In fact, they just more or less tried to deny that there was anything out of the ordinary going on with their kids' lives—except to play a kind of "swat-the-fly" game continually with each other. Deb would try to "bother" Kurt with a concern, like a fly buzzing around his head, and Kurt would "swat" her down with his domineering ways.

When Vicki married a drug-addicted man after college graduation, Kurt, Deb, and their respective spouses were present, smiling and oblivious to anything being out of place.

When Adam dropped out of college Kurt blamed Deb. Deb blamed Kurt. And the broken family network perpetuated its misery and loneliness to the next generation through Vicki's three children of divorce and the two children Adam had with a girl out-of-wedlock and deserted.

The Different Faces of Loneliness

We've seen that loneliness can be a burdensome influence whether it strikes a child or adult, alone, in a crowd, or in the midst of conflict. Loneliness can take on many forms and infiltrate the lives of those it haunts like a heavy fog at night. It can be the root problem of many other outwardly manifested symptoms.

Loneliness can wear the faces of other emotions and mask itself very well sometimes. Kurt's loneliness showed itself in a defensive, angry power trip. Deb's loneliness presented itself in her insecure, irrational panic. Vicki's loneliness caused her to withdraw. Adam's loneliness and chaotic emotions tumbled out from within the Sleeper Effect Syndrome.

Later, as the family network became more and more crippled, loneliness pushed Kurt and Deb into the depths of denial. It drove Vicki and Adam to seek solace from their pain in alcohol and drugs.

The ironic thing about loneliness is that it never stays alone—a variety of other miserable problems usually travel right along with it!

MANAGEMENT: LEARNING TO ALLOW YOURSELF JOY

To really allow yourself the joy of living, it is imperative for you to accept that negative emotions are very powerful. One shout of misplaced anger can undo an entire day of pleasantness. One outbreak of venomous hate can rattle destructively through a family network for weeks or months. If negative emotions are vented at the wrong time or in the wrong way, an undercurrent of resentment, bitterness, and rage can simmer for long periods of time. These negative emotions are so powerful they can penetrate every corner of a person and his/her relationships.

Negative emotions alienate us from one another. Loneliness then comes scurrying along through the door we leave open for it. Once loneliness has taken up residence it can be very difficult to evict.

Adult children of divorce are especially vulnerable to the long term effects of negative emotions. Many of these powerful feelings may have been building up momentum since childhood to be unleashed eventually on other significant people who really had nothing to do with the negative emotions in the first place.

What Can You Do?

First, recognize that negative emotions are extremely powerful if you leave them to their own devices.

Second, get rid of them! In fact, Ephesians 4:31 says, "Get rid of all bitterness, rage, and anger, brawling, and slander along with every form of malice."

Getting rid of negative emotions takes planning, effort, creative energy, contemplation, and practice! You are not likely to wake up one day and find that you no longer have negative emotions. It's more a matter of being prepared to get rid of them constructively as they come upon you throughout your lifetime.

Some of the following suggestions may help you to begin to more easily and consciously get rid of powerful negative emotions such as loneliness:

1. Extend your hand first—provide an opportunity to bring an issue into the open or clear up a misunderstanding by

stating exactly what you're feeling *in a non-bl*aming way. For instance, you may say, "I feel hurt about not being remembered on my birthday." Don't say, "Because you didn't remember my birthday I have to feel this hurt!" Rather than saying, "I'm sorry you misunderstood what I felt and you got me so upset I said hateful things," say, "I am sorry that I was so upset I said hateful things."

2. Receive from others — allow others to indicate how they feel and allow them to love you, care about you or communicate with you without turning your back. Receiving can be a very uncomfortable thing. If you've had an argument with your spouse or been shunned by a co-worker it may be difficult for you to notice their offerings to make peace and even more difficult to receive them.

For example, if your spouse has a hard time expressing regret, and you know this to be true, you may need to be more receptive to his/her individual way of saying, "I'm sorry." A compliment, a small gift or a quick smile may mean, "I'm sorry." No, you shouldn't have to be a mind reader, but people are all different and if you're truly going to get rid of negative emotions you may have to fine-tune your emotional antennae and be prepared to receive positive messages. Receive other people's positive actions and feelings graciously by becoming more aware of how they communicate.

3. Get rid of powerful negative emotions by becoming involved in group activities. Joining a health club, a volleyball league, bowling team, or Bible study will help to draw you outside of yourself, focus on other people's perspectives, minimize the amount of priority you've given your negative emotions, and maximize the opportunity for negative emotions to dissipate. For instance, if you've had a tough encounter with a friend or one of your children, and you go out to lunch with an upbeat group of acquaintances, you may find that your irritation or hurt feelings are gone afterward. Don't allow negative emotions to get bigger than they need to be.

4. Disallow powerful negative emotions by accepting that you are unique in your needs, ideas, feelings, attitudes, idiosyn-

crasies, and pressures. You will not always be affected in the same way as the next guy by the same situation. You may not even be affected the same way by the same issue on two different occasions yourself!

Your mother may feel slighted on Sunday by a comment your grandma made. It may not bother you at all. But had the same comment been on Thursday, it may have bothered you terribly and flown right by your mother. You are a complex set of unique needs.

But you're also the same as others too. It can help to rid yourself of negative emotions by remembering this as well. You hurt, cry, laugh, feel humiliated, get afraid, and rejoice over life's happenings in much the same way as other people. Maybe you don't cry at weddings, but it doesn't mean you don't feel as happy as the next person in attendance.

Accept your uniqueness. Accept your sameness. And you can help diminish the power which negative emotions have in your life.

5. Know that everyone has days when he feels like "the odd man out." You are not the only one who gets dumped on by others or who has bad breaks! Other people have moments when they feel left on life's sidelines while everybody else is playing in the game. If you realize you are not the only one who goes through difficulties, challenges, and dark emotions, you can help to immobilize the power of negative emotions— especially self-pity and loneliness!

For example, realizing that the neighbors next door have conflict too can help keep you from feeling overwhelmed by anger and resentment—spreading out the negative makes it less effective!

6. Accept the hand that God extends to help you. Philippians 4:6-7 says, "Do not be anxious about anything, but in everything, by prayer and petition, with thanksgiving, present your requests to God. And the peace of God, which transcends all understanding, will guard your hearts and your minds in Christ Jesus."

The peace of God transcends, or surpasses, all understanding. You may think you've been hurt, angered, or embittered so deeply that nothing will help your loneliness. But prayer is your twenty-four-hour link with the peace of God, which is more powerful *than* any negative emotion.

Sometimes, doing the opposite of what our human minds think we should do is exactly what we need to do. For example, as a result of growing up in a divorced family, you may think you can never stop hating or hurting, and that it's a sign of weakness or helplessness to hand your problems over to God. But if you can pray, "Thank You, Lord, for allowing me the challenge to overcome my problems. Please give me the strength, knowledge, wisdom, and understanding to do so," you may be absolutely amazed at how quickly and thoroughly you begin to find ways to solve your problems.

The circumstances of your past can't be changed. But how you look at them, feel about them—and use—them can! Transforming deeply rooted and powerful negative influences and experiences in life into beneficial, strengthening wholeness is the very business that God is in!

Being Accountable for Your Own Happiness

A prominent risk for ACDs is to allow the conflict and negative emotions of parents' divorce to be crutches of blame to lean on. Adult children of divorce can run a dangerous course of blame that keeps them stuck in a rut on the way to becoming a fully functioning adult.

You can blame everything—from the way you frown to a fear of locked doors—on your parents. It will never change the fact that at some point in your life you will have to move onward, beyond blame, in order to be an adult with a fulfilling, happy life.

At some point it is necessary to say, "Okay, I understand myself better for working through the negative effects of living in a divorced family network. I'm a stronger, healthier person now. The past is gone, I cannot change it. I must have the courage to be accountable for my own choices and happiness."

Even if your parents beat each other and you; even if you were sexually molested; even if you were ridiculed, criticized, and harped on to the point of zero self-esteem; and even if your parents both abandoned you physically and/or emotionally, you alone can take responsibility for putting the pieces of your life together and going on.

Nobody else can call a counselor, support group, doctor, pastor, or friend in search of help. Nobody else can force you to take any of the steps offered in this book to help you. Nobody else can make you *pray*. You must do it! And you can. Inner joy springs from a bottomless well of love, strength, peace, adaptability, faith, hope, courage, wisdom, knowledge, understanding, and mercy. You are allowed to drink from this well. There is nobody who's had it so tough, nobody who is so oppressed, or nobody who's been so bad that they can't drink from the bottomless well of God's love.

In John 4:14 Jesus tells us, "Whoever drinks the water I give him will never thirst. Indeed, the water I give him will become in him a spring of water welling up to eternal life."

You have a choice about your life. You can allow the bitterness, anger, hatred, resentment, strife, and loneliness you've suffered to overwhelm you. You can blame your problems on your parents, siblings, extended families, stepfamilies, husbands, wives, children, employers, or friends. But in the end, only you can account for your choices, attitudes, feelings, actions, and happiness. You can be led by others to the wellspring of inner joy, but they can't drink for you!

If you are deeply enmeshed with negative emotions, write down the steps listed here to help you get out of their grasp. Put it where you can see it every day:

1. Extend your hand first.
2. Receive from others.
3. Get involved in group activities.
4. Accept your uniqueness/accept your sameness.
5. Know that everyone has moments of feeling like the "Odd Man Out."

6. Take the hand that God extends.
7. Be accountable for your life.
8. Drink from the wellspring of inner joy.

These steps may help to diminish the power of negative emotions in your life. If you are in the tight grip of loneliness, however, you may also find the following exercise useful.

Exercise: Jumping into Life

When you're lonely it can seem almost impossible to jump into the mainstream of life. Everywhere you look other people are having fun and enjoying life. But not you! The "happy" people are having fun and enjoying life, but not you! The "happy" people are lunching, brunching, and playing tennis or golf. The "happy" people are skiing, backpacking, and going on trips. But not you—you're home watching television every night or walking through a mall seeing how happy everyone else is.

What you may forget is that of the two ladies chatting away by the lemonade stand, one may be relating how her husband's chemotherapy is going. The guy smiling at the clerk in the pet store may be buying a puppy for his grandson who just broke a leg and can't play the rest of the football season. The beautician cutting a young boy's hair may have just found out her mother has Alzheimer's disease. And your parents went through a nightmarish divorce when you were young.

Life goes on. Just like you, those people you see who seem so happy have problems and emotional scars. They may not be the exact same ones, but they are as painful to them in their own way. You must take responsibility to jump into life and begin interacting with people. To eliminate your loneliness, you must act like a person who isn't lonely. You must take the first steps to reach outside of yourself.

Each day for six weeks do two of the following exercises and write down in a spiral notebook or diary how you felt before, during, and after the occasion:

1. Telephone a friend or loved one who lives nearby.
2. Write a note to a friend or loved one who lives far away.
3. Invite an acquaintance or co-worker for lunch.
4. Window shop for something that forces you to interact with a salesperson — a car, clothes, sporting goods, etc.
5. Talk with the clerks in stores, banks, etc.
6. Talk to the postal clerk when you buy stamps.
7. Go to church or join a Bible study.
8. Choose a hobby and join a related club.
9. Volunteer to work with a social service organization.
10. Join a local sports club, league, or community team.
11. Go to a park and strike up a conversation.
12. Visit museums, zoos, trade shows, conventions, etc. and talk to those working there about their products or services.
13. Become a Scout or 4-H leader.
14. Go next door and greet (or meet) your neighbors.
15. Go to the humane society and discuss a pet that may be just right for you.

At the end of your six weeks read back over what your experiences felt like. Did they feel increasingly more enjoyable? Do any bring pleasant memories to mind? Are you challenging yourself to do braver things? If so, great! Keep going, add more things to your list until you find you don't feel haunted by loneliness anymore!

When we are greatly influenced by negative emotions, particularly loneliness, we often find ourselves falling victim or giving way to physical ailments. It is an undeniable fact that if our emotional, mental, and spiritual well-being are out of sync, our physical health will be affected. In the next chapter, we'll look at some of the causes of physical ailments and how we can cope with them, as well as emotional drain.

-9-

Physical Ailments and Emotional Drain

There are times in our lives when everything piles up to the point that we need to "hibernate" for a few days. Often after final exams at college, a long-awaited vacation, a cherished wedding celebration, job promotion, a move, or an important goal is met, we find ourselves with a cold, the flu, facial break-out, strained back, or some other temporary physical setback.

Stress is stress—whether it's good or bad. Sometimes we get through the long haul on an extra amount of adrenaline that gives us more energy, more tolerance for pain, or more ability to shuffle life around for awhile. But during an ordeal—good or bad—we use up more of ourselves.

When the party's over, the test taken, or the contract signed, we relax. And whatever germs our systems have been suppressing, or strain that's been coming on is quietly wait-ing—ready to pounce. This is partially due to immune systems that aren't as alert or hearty as usual, but also it may be a self-preservation course that needs to be run.

Little kids will usually go and go until an adult forces them to rest or they drop from exhaustion. Adults are the same, except they must monitor their own schedules. If an adult won't (or temporarily can't) take good care of his physical health in the midst of extra stress—he will stop eventually—it may be from exhaustion, however.

A tired mind and body allows all sorts of funny things to happen. You may get migraine headaches, diarrhea, constipation, nausea, colon spasms, chest pains, adult acne, and strained (or tensed) muscles. These, along with a myriad of other symptoms, all walk a closely connected line with stress.

It's always safest to check with a medical doctor when you have any unusual symptoms. These same stress-related symptoms can also mean the onset of a serious illness. If you're having any funny aches, pains, or feelings, take the time and spend the money to get a check-up! You're worth it. Your body is a very finely tuned "machine." Just as an odd noise in the car will most likely require a mechanic's attention, aches and pains will eventually drive us to the doctor, but it's usually much less painful and costly to go for routine maintenance than for a complete fix-up!

Delayed Reactions

Sometimes physical ailments will come immediately following a crisis or a time of rejoicing. But other times, especially when we're forced to get on with the business of living, we keep going for weeks, months, or even years before a specific emotional stress, long-term anxiety, suppressed anger, guilt or shame, feelings of helplessness, loneliness, resentment, or despair, and the ravages of depression show outwardly in physical symptoms. Adult children of divorce, especially, may have to take a hard, honest look at stress-related symptoms and delve into their past to track down possible sources of their ailments. Sometimes they form reactive habits such as long-term fatigue, disturbed sleep patterns, and lethargy, all left over from childhood. For instance, during her parents' divorce a child may be extremely overburdened with doing housework, caring for younger siblings, and keeping up with a hectic activity schedule; she may have frequent stomachaches or leg cramps due to the extra heavy load. Subconsciously, as she matures into adulthood, she develops a "programed response" of reacting with these same symptoms when her life is under too much pressure.

As a child a young man may learn to keep his thoughts and feelings to himself. His powerful fears, doubts, anger, guilt, and other negative emotions may "come out" in the form of severe headaches or odd sleep disturbances. As an adult he may very well have similar symptoms when an emotional crisis happens or he continues to suppress "old" problems.

If you have a sore and you keep scraping away the new skin that's trying to form, the sore simply won't heal. If you keep irritating it and new bacteria comes in contact with it, you may get a very serious infection. This infection may go much deeper than you can see on the surface. It may taint the entire blood system. Emotional problems can do the same thing.

As an adult you may constantly bicker and argue with your children about their overfilled schedules, getting to bed on time, or staying away from home too much. That's the surface irritation. But the real "infection" may lie in the vow you subconsciously made that *your* kids won't be run so ragged that they succumb to the same kind of lethargy and depression you lived with after your parents' divorce.

Holding Back Can Keep You Down

Inhibitions about sex, trying new things, socializing, profanity, and any number of other aspects of your life may be a physical burden to you too. One ACD got a pinch in her stomach when she heard someone curse. It reminded her Piggy-Back Child of her father and mother screaming obscenities at each other. Another ACD had severe problems with impotence because (as he discovered through extensive therapy) he was so repulsed by hearing his mother in her bedroom next to his in sexual situations with different men when he was a little boy.

Yet another ACD would get diarrhea and panic attacks the night before a planned excursion for fun and relaxation. This man realized (again after therapy) that he was so inhibited that he could hardly function in social or "adventuring" circumstances because of the great impact his fighting parents had on him as a child during and after their divorce. It seemed to him that every time he was with his parents in public, they fought, made an embarrassing scene, and ended up hating each other more. His deep inner fear was that leaving home meant purposefully seeking or risking unpleasantness. So, his Piggy-Back Child tried to keep him home with physical ailments.

We do well to remember our minds are so powerful and complex that everything we experience is tucked away somewhere for as long as we live. It may be exhausting to try to figure out and analyze every little thing we do. It really doesn't matter so much why we get a warm feeling every time a song comes on the radio, or why we refuse to clean the bathroom without rubber gloves—these don't change the course of our lives. But it *does* matter why we will or will not do things because we get such overt physical symptoms that we can't function.

If you get nauseated every time someone shouts in your presence, it will most likely be helpful if you determine why. You may discover it is because when your parents shouted at home it meant serious trouble would follow. Then you can work on re-programing your response as an adult and help to calm your Piggy-Back Child.

It would be just plain silly to deny that all the experiences our minds retain don't affect how we behave and respond to certain situations as adults. It is our responsibility as adults to integrate our conscious choices and behaviors with the powerful direction of our subconscious minds. If we don't, we automatically choose to live under the tyranny of our Piggy-Back Children, and we will subordinate our joy in life to their irrational dictatorships.

MANAGEMENT: BECOMING HEALTHY

Michelle went to Dr. Barrows with heart palpitations, burning sensations in her stomach, and complaints of frequent diarrhea. Dr. Barrows ordered a battery of various tests. Nothing physiological showed up to indicate that anything was out of the ordinary.

Michelle asked, "What is wrong with me, Doctor? Do I have cancer or something else serious that just can't be seen yet?"

Dr. Barrows smiled, "I doubt it, Michelle. Of course, we must discuss your symptoms thoroughly and possibly order more tests to rule out other possibilities. But I think we'll proceed with a lengthy consultation first. Why don't you make another appointment to see me next week? In between, keep a list of anything that happens just before and after your symptoms. For example, did you have an argument with your husband, do strenuous exercise, or have symptoms before or after you ate?

"Keep track of these and note any other pertinent thoughts that come to mind. Then we'll see if we can draw any parallels or associations."

Michelle did specifically what Dr. Barrows asked her to do. Meticulously, all week long, she kept records of what happened before every ache, pain, or other symptom. When Dr. Barrows examined the list she was not surprised.

"Okay, Michelle," Dr. Barrows began, "you tell me if you notice any particular connections between your physical problems and your daily habits."

Michelle had been considering this very thing all week and didn't have any solid conclusions. However, she did have some uneasy suspicions. Now, she shrugged, "I guess the only thing I see clearly is that there's nothing clear for a pattern! I thought I might turn up with an allergy, ulcer, or something specific, but I sure didn't!"

"I agree that there isn't a pattern here to indicate exact physical problems, Michelle. But I disagree that there is no clear pattern. I do see some consistencies in your list."

"You do?" Michelle was almost relieved. It was agony to have physical aches and pains and not know what was causing them. "What are they?"

"Well," Dr. Barrows answered, "I'd like to ask you a few questions before we get to that. For instance, are you a heavy coffee drinker?" Michelle nodded. Dr. Barrows made a note, "Do you smoke?" Michelle shook her head.

Dr. Barrows made another note. She asked, "Has anything unusual been going on at home recently?"

Michelle was quick to reply, "It's not just stress, Doctor."

"I didn't say anything about stress. What makes you answer with that so fast?"

Michelle pursed her lips and shook her head in irritation. "Because Jerry keeps telling me my physical problems are all in my head. And I keep telling him I'm not going nuts!"

Dr. Barrows made another note and asked, "Does Jerry say that you're 'nuts'?"

"Not in those words. He says I'm stressed-out and psychosomatic. Why do you want to know?"

"Because it would seem to me to be fairly challenging to get along with a husband who said you were nuts," Dr. Barrows ventured.

"Ha!" Michelle exclaimed. "He's such a perfectionist, he wouldn't stay with a wife who was nuts!"

"What makes you call Jerry a perfectionist?" Dr. Barrows probed.

"Oh, I don't know," Michelle said cynically. "Maybe it's that he makes sure all his shoes are lined up in the closet perfectly every night or that he wants me to vacuum the carpet every single day. Or, it could be that he won't ever think of leaving the car outside the garage for the night. Then there's the way I fold clothes—it's always been wrong. Does that give you any clues?"

Dr. Barrows smiled, "So, Jerry puts quite a bit of pressure on you to do things his way?"

Michelle shrugged, "Well, I try hard to do things the way he wants just to have peace at home. I mean, if I didn't pick up after the kids, or if Jerry ever saw how they can leave a bathroom after a shower, there'd be war for days!"

"So you clean up behind the kids," Dr. Barrows stated. "It must be hard to keep up with a house, job, marriage, kids, and still find time for yourself."

"Oh, I don't take any time for myself," Michelle said seriously. "The whole family would fall apart if I did!"

"Why do you think that, Michelle?"

Michelle laughed, "Because if I did anything on my own nobody could stand it! Jerry would be crazy with jealousy, the kids would be running wild, the house would turn into a shambles — and I'd never get caught up again! The only time I can wash the kitchen floor now is at midnight when everyone else is in bed."

"Do you stay up late on your own quite often?" Dr. Barrows asked, making another note on the paper Michelle had given to her.

"Yes, it's the only time I do have alone."

"That must be hard on your private relationship with Jerry."

"You mean our sex life," Michelle said matter-of-factly. "We haven't really had one for the last few years."

"Oh?" Dr. Barrows raised her eyebrows. "Why not?"

"Life just got busy, I guess. Jerry works, I work, the kids need a lot of our attention — something's gotta give."

"Hmm." Dr. Barrows tapped the eraser of her pencil against her chin. "Michelle, do you resent Jerry for being a perfectionist?"

"Do you mean do I withhold sex from him as punishment?"

"You're a very astute patient, Michelle. Yes, that could be one expression of resentment. But I mean more in general."

"About the only thing I can think of that I really resent Jerry for is that he's just like my dad — but then Jerry can't help that."

Dr. Barrows made yet another note and asked, "Don't you get along with your father?"

"Not really," Michelle admitted. "Actually, he's kind of a jerk! A big jerk, now that I think of it!"

"How so?" Dr. Barrows queried.

"Let's see, where shall I start?" Michelle rolled her eyes. "First, he left my mother when I was three. They divorced. Then they remarried when I was about to start kindergarten. Then my mother kicked him out when I was seven. He was so mad he did all sorts of rotten things."

"Like what?" Dr. Barrows asked.

"Like calling in the middle of the night and screaming at my mom over the phone. And blocking Mom's car in the driveway so she couldn't get out. He kidnaped me after school twice—and wouldn't give me back until Mom agreed to go out on dates with him."

"Did he stop doing such things after awhile?"

"Not really. My mom remarried a great guy when I was nine. I loved my stepfather immediately. In fact, when I got married I had him walk me down the aisle. I didn't even invite my dad to my wedding!"

"But you mentioned your dad didn't really stop doing inappropriate things. What did you mean?"

"To this day, my dad still makes annoying phone calls to my mom. Mostly though, he transferred his 'jerk attacks' to me. He bombs over to my house at all times of the day and night— whenever he feels like it—and just hangs around. He thinks we'll stop whatever we're doing to entertain him!" Michelle said in exasperation.

"Do you?" Dr. Barrows asked point blank.

Michelle looked startled, "Uh—uh—well, yes! I guess we do. I mean, he's such a presence. If he's around, everyone knows about it. If you don't kowtow to his every request or laugh at his dumb jokes, he acts like a spoiled brat! Once, he threatened to call my boss and tell him I wasn't really home ill— and I was! That's my dad's idea of funny!"

"Amazing," Dr. Barrows shook her head. "But what I'm really concerned about is that you feel your husband is like your father."

"Yeah," Michelle acknowledged. "I'm afraid in a lot of ways, he is."

"Have you ever considered divorcing Jerry?" Dr. Barrows asked.

"No way!" Michelle raised her voice. "If I did that he'd haunt me for the rest of my life, and then I'd have two ghosts on my hands!"

There's No Shame in Stress-Related Physical Ailments

Eventually Dr. Barrows and Michelle agreed that Michelle should see a counselor regularly. They also agreed that Michelle's symptoms were, in fact, stress-related. When all the notes which Dr. Barrows took were collected, they showed a clear pattern.

Michelle got up in a rush each morning, skipped breakfast, gulped down two or three cups of coffee, made sure Jerry and the kids had their breakfasts, saw everyone else off to their destinations, went to work herself, drank coffee off and on until lunch, grabbed a quick lettuce salad, went back to work, drank coffee all afternoon, did errands on the way home from work, started hearing about the kids' day as she came through the doorway, put on another pot of coffee as she listened to Jerry's day, fixed dinner, had more coffee as she folded clothes or supervised homework, put the kids to bed, said good night to Jerry, cleaned up the house or took care of other miscellaneous responsibilities, went to bed herself, and did the same things all over the next day.

Dr. Barrows bluntly concluded that keeping up this kind of pace on top of contending with what she saw as some potentially lethal inner emotional turbulence was definitely contributing to Michelle's physical symptoms. Michelle reluctantly agreed and consented to begin the weekly appointments with a counselor Dr. Barrows recommended.

But Dr. Barrows also advised Michelle on some ways she could begin to take better care of herself and start to become healthier:

1. Proper rest — Dr. Barrows suggested that Michelle be in bed by 10:00 or 11:00 P.M. no matter what jobs were left undone around the house. If Michelle and Jerry didn't feel like talking or snuggling, then she should read a relaxing book, but she needed better rest!

2. Proper diet — the first thing Dr. Barrows told Michelle was to stop drinking so much coffee. She recommended that Michelle look up articles about the side effects of too much

caffeine. She suggested medical books and magazines available at the library. The second thing was for Michelle to eat something nutritious for breakfast. If it had to be quick it could be healthy muffins, whole grain cereal, yogurt, cheese, fruit, etc.

And the third thing was to try to eat a variety of foods at lunch time. One lettuce salad between dinner one evening and dinner the next was *not* a well-balanced diet!

3. Proper Exercise — Dr. Barrows pointed out that running after a family and around at work was not an adequate form of exercise for Michelle.

Michelle could join an aerobics class three afternoons or evenings a week and finally take some time for herself. Or, she could set time aside at home and do aerobics along with a videotape. Michelle should walk, jog, bike, or swim — something purposefully physical — for at least half an hour at a time, three days each week.

4. Finally, Dr. Barrows prescribed that Michelle rent a comedy video movie to watch at some time during each week. It could be one for the whole family, for just Jerry and Michelle, or just for Michelle. But it had to be funny! Dr. Barrows told Michelle that it was essential to balance the seriousness and hectic pace of today's life with a healthy dose of humor, and this seemed especially vital in Michelle's case.

Dr. Barrows sent Michelle off with a warm handshake and told her she would like to see her in a month to check on how she was feeling and doing.

Good Therapy Really Helps

After only four sessions with the counselor, Michelle had tremendous news to report to Dr. Barrows at her next appointment. Dr. Barrows had barely sat down on her swivel stool before Michelle bubbled, "You can't believe how much poison is coming out in my counseling sessions, Doctor!"

"Oh?" Dr. Barrows was somewhat stunned at Michelle's bluntness. "Tell me more."

"Well, in the first place," Michelle began enthusiastically,

"I do have bunches and bunches of resentment about my relationships with my dad, my husband, and about my parents' divorce that I've stuffed inside."

"Did the counselor tell you that?" Dr. Barrows questioned warily.

"Oh, no!" Michelle grinned. "She doesn't tell me any-thing—she asks me questions that lead me to tell myself! I think what's happened is this. I got so full of all the frustration, bitterness, resentment, and other icky things that I wouldn't face that it could come out in physical symptoms. I helped give the emotions an easy outlet by not taking care of myself!"

"What a wonderful discovery!" Dr. Barrows said suppor-tively.

"Oh, yes," Michelle nodded her head excitedly. "You can't believe how much progress I'm making. I must have been at just the right place in my life to leap forward so quickly. Twice this month I've told my dad he'd have to go home because we had other plans. He was so shocked he actually left without a fuss! It felt so good to take some control over my own life for a change."

Dr. Barrows thought Michelle would burst in her new-found freedom. "What else?" she prodded.

"Umm!" Michelle cooed. "I've been eating better, resting better, exercising, and watching a comedy every week just as you said. I feel so-o-o much better. I'm having a tough time cutting out the coffee though. The first few days I thought my head would split! But I found out that most of my physical symptoms came after I'd drunk several cups of coffee, and from what I looked up in the medical dictionary, that's par for the course! So, I have to devise a plan to wean myself from the coffee and still function with the withdrawal!"

Dr. Barrows smiled, "I think you'll manage. Anything new with you, Jerry, and the kids?"

"Uh-huh!" Michelle enthused. "I let the kids' rooms go all last week and made rules. What they don't clean up, pick up, or throw in the dirty laundry gets put in a 'Lost and Found' closet—they lost it, I found it, and I'll decide what to do with it. Of course they didn't really believe me at first. But every day I found something out of place I put it in the closet. When my youngest lost his favorite red truck, that was it. Their rooms have been spotless for three days in a row."

Michelle looked sheepish as she continued, "I wouldn't care so much about the rooms, but it was the only way I could think of to please Jerry's pickiness and my need to let up a little. Pretty soon I'm going to have the courage to explain the whole thing to Jerry—he doesn't even know my closet plan yet—and turn the responsibility for the kids' rooms over to him. If he wants them to be so tidy, he can deal with it!"

"What progress!" Dr. Barrows affirmed. "And what about Jerry? Any insights about your marriage?"

Michelle looked down at the floor, "Not exactly anything with Jerry. He thought I was awful to send my father away. And he complained that the dinner dishes weren't done a few mornings. But I'm practicing thinking 'Healthy Thoughts' in that department."

Dr. Barrows looked up questioningly and Michelle went on, "I'm taking each day separately and thinking of things that Jerry does that are good and positive. One day all I could think of was that he had to go to an evening meeting and I'd have a couple hours free from the sour attitude he'd had that afternoon."

Michelle screwed up her face into a sort of grimace. "I'm trying to replace my automatic 'He's such a jerk like my father' response with, 'He's a different human being than my father,' and, 'There are things I love about Jerry—otherwise I wouldn't have married him!'"

"Sounds reasonable," Dr. Barrows acknowledged. "Is it working?"

"A little. I have longer moments in the same room with Jerry when I don't tense my jaw or clench my fists. One day at a time. And I am getting so much out of therapy. I just didn't realize how much major life crises—like my parents' divorce—could affect me, and for such a long period of time!"

Dr. Barrows agreed completely, "Sometimes it's very difficult to make a connection between heartburn and heartache. But, unless there's a specific indication associated with disease, injury, infection, or other physical trauma, a doctor usually tries at least to consider a patient's emotional health. In your case, you made my job easy."

"Well," Michelle stated, "it's turning out to be the best discovery I've ever made. I've discovered me! And I'm adopting a new policy for my life. 'If something can't seriously hurt or kill me or somebody else, I'm going to go for it!' I've always wanted to take up a couple of hobbies and I'm going to follow through. It won't hurt Jerry and the kids to have me gone once in awhile or to get their own dinner!"

Dr. Barrows was very pleased with the change in Michelle's attitude. It was as if she had unlocked chains that had been holding her down. Some of those chains were so long, they reached clear into her past to when she was a little girl suffering through the trauma of her parents' two divorces and the ensuing problems.

Before Michelle left, she and Dr. Barrows quickly went over a list of Michelle's prescribed treatment.

Physical Problems: Sound Solutions

1. Keep a list of any ongoing or new physical symptoms you may have. Write down what they are, when they occur, and what may be happening in conjunction with them.
2. Take this record to a medical doctor and get a thorough physical examination.
3. Consider stress-related and emotional problems as contributing factors to any physical problems.
4. Discuss your problems openly with a professional doctor, counselor, pastor, or other reputable caregiver with whom you are comfortable.
5. Take good care of yourself: get proper rest, diet and exercise.
6. Get plenty of humor and laughter in your life.
7. Be creative in thinking of healthy solutions and compromises to resolve problems.
8. Think healthy thoughts.

9. Nurture yourself. If it's not going to seriously hurt or kill you or somebody else—go for it!

Getting healthy and staying that way can be much more difficult than it sounds. The next exercise may further help you to chart a course for your individual needs.

EXERCISE: CHARTING GOALS FOR YOUR WELL-BEING

Physical health is a combination of mental, emotional, spiritual, and bodily well-being. You can chart your way to health if you, as Dr. Robert Schuller says, "Plan your work and work your plan—if you are failing to plan, you are planning to fail!"[1] The following simple process, kept in a folder that you work from *each* day, will help you to keep your well-being a top priority. Write or type the list of items that follow. Make several copies of this sheet. Then take the first sheet and check off each item as you take care of it *every* day. This provides an "accountability-to-yourself" system that helps you see at a glance whether or not you are nurturing your well-being.

What I Have Done Good Today Toward My Well Being

Body: Ate right
Exercised
Drank 8—10 glasses of water
Rested well last night

Mind: Considered something I'd like to improve on
Pleasant thoughts about life
Challenged myself with a new idea/concept
Read something
Asked a question and got an answer

Heart: Told someone I loved them
Gave someone a compliment
Smiled at someone I didn't know

Told myself I was a good person
Thought of a lovable thing about myself

Soul: Read in the Bible
Prayed
Asked someone a question about God
Expressed a thought about God to someone
(or wrote it down in a journal)
Thanked God for my life

Stick to this plan — you may have arthritis, a bad back, or a heart problem, but if you can tend to the four areas of physical health you will inevitably become a better, healthier person!

As you chart a healthy course for yourself you may be tempted to try to control life itself rather than taking control of your life. Next we will look at how easy it is for adult children of divorce to fall into a dangerous life trap — an unhealthy quest for control. We'll also look at ways to balance and manage problems that can help to free you from this trap.

-10-

The Quest for Control

Sometimes, when things are clicking along smoothly for us, we can almost convince ourselves that we've stumbled upon a "magic recipe" for happiness and that things such as divorce, illness, tragedy, and other difficulties won't visit our lives.

Often, we go even further and seemingly operate from a belief that if we can control our circumstances we can "force happiness to live with us!"

For some reason, even though we see people all around us fall victim to time and unforeseen calamities, we still hold tenaciously to the hope that if we just have enough money, good looks, a better house, a more fulfilling job, or well-laid plans we can become charter members of the "magic recipe club" and completely control how our lives turn out.

There's almost a conviction that says, "I know that Eden is out there for me. It's just a matter of getting things lined up right and in control before I find it." It's as if there's something we can *do* in our lifetimes to ensure our success and happiness.

Inwardly, when push comes to shove, most of us do have a sense of the reality that there are no guarantees in life. The multi-billionaire can lose his material possessions. The loving couple can be tragically torn apart by death. The strong, healthy athlete can be cut down in his prime by illness or accident. Little children can become victims of their parents' vicious divorces.

ACDs can be particularly vulnerable to the quicksands of belief that there is a "magic recipe" to find and follow. You may want to believe so badly that your parents couldn't put their family through so much pain and heartbreak that you choose to try to control your life from this point onward. It could come to the place where everything that's happened and everything that "will be" has to come out "all right."

Instead of taking control of your life you are trying to control life itself, and this is impossible. It's like trying to stop the moon from getting full or the tide from coming in — it can't be done.

Following are several traits that ACDs commonly exhibit in one form or another in their often desperate quest to control life. Do you:

1. Deny that your parents' divorce affected you at all?
2. Blame your parents' divorce for every problem you have as an adult?
3. Surround yourself with people who are harsh, judgmental, nonaffectionate, unloving, and critical because you expect no more from your fellow humans?
4. Keep your spouse and other significant people in the dark and unenlightened regarding your self-discoveries? This way you can manipulate them. You fear that if others grow and mature they will no longer find you an acceptable partner, friend, or relative, or that you will no longer be one.
5. Refuse to discuss your family's history, faults, or weaknesses, because it is malicious to gossip outside

the family network? This way you don't have to understand yourself better and desensitize yourself to the impact of your parents' divorce.

6. Refuse to accept that, regardless of what went on in childhood, your parents are still your parents, you are still their offspring, and there will be shadows to live with in your life, just as everybody else has in theirs?

7. Hang on to the idea that you have to live in the highest lifestyle, the best home or the finest neighborhood to prove you're in control of life?

8. Reject the idea that contentment during the ambitious journey is a key to staying in self-balance?

9. Shy away from demanding excellence from yourself in whatever place you are in life right now — always putting off doing your best for later?

10. Fall prey to the false god of money-love? Money allows you to buy your way out of meeting yourself or God toe-to-toe. Putting money first means you don't have to be an excellent person because you can buy excellent things.

11. Withhold forgiveness from your parents or others who've hurt you because if you forgive them you would have to be accountable for your own well-being and confront "messy" emotions?

12. Back away from achievement because challenging yourself results in you being challenged by haunting things such as anxiety, fear, doubt, and rejection?

13. Seek success consistently to the point of "almost" and then fail because success requires excellence and ACDs don't always believe that excellence exists?

These are all control issues you use to control either yourself or those around you! Quite often we think of control in terms of aggression. And, yes, ACDs can have problems with acting out aggressions they absorbed or learned as children of divorce. But, more typically, ACDs control through intricate and subtle means. Because mistrust can be such an issue for adult children of divorce, you may develop an early life habit of orchestrating situations from behind "psychological scenes."

An ACD may very well appear to be supple, useable, and easily placated all the while he or she is kneading people and situations to exercise control. Greg is like this. He's thirty-eight and appears to be an easy-going, unassuming sort. He, like so many adult children of divorce, reached the point where his first marriage was no longer healthy or functioning, and it ended in divorce. He's been going steady with Ellen, thirty-two and never married, for several months now. He loves her in his way, but inwardly Greg is frightened of a "permanent" commitment — that probably wouldn't be permanent anyway, as Greg sees it.

For all his seeming gentle nature, Greg actually has a nearly unquenchable thirst for control. When he recognizes "emotional places he's been before" from his marriage, he manipulates Ellen right in or out of the situations.

Greg was six when his parents divorced, and he was devastated. His mother moved him and his two siblings out of the house Greg's father had inherited from his own parents.

Having been used to a beautiful home, a large spending allowance, and lots of leisure time during the day as a stay-at-home-mom, it was very hard on Greg's mother's pride to fall victim to another common problem of women and children of divorce — an extremely lower standard of living.

Greg's father had an exceptionally competent accountant and a very bright attorney. Between the two, it was proven to the court's satisfaction that Greg's father could not afford to support his ex-wife and children in the manner to which they were accustomed. Greg's mother had to move herself and her three children into a tiny, two-bedroom house with one bathroom.

Greg still remembers staring out of the window of the bedroom he shared with his older brother, longing for the space and freedom of the old house with four bedrooms and three bathrooms. Now, he had to take his turn in the bathroom each morning, after his mother and brother, but before his younger sister. There weren't any extra rooms to play in or any yards to explore. Even at six, Greg wondered why his dad needed the whole big house to himself. Greg supposed his mother was right—his father was just plain mean.

Greg's mother became a receptionist. Several months later she married her boss. The three children moved into a big house again—with their mother and her new husband.

Greg's older brother was going to be nine soon. He did not like his stepfather at all. And on a visit to his father's house he begged to move back "home." But his father explained to the kids that he couldn't possibly take on all three of them alone, and it wouldn't be fair to choose only one child to live with him.

Greg wondered how his mother could take on all three kids, but his father couldn't. He supposed his mother was right—his father was just plain selfish.

After that, Greg's older brother became very aggressive and antagonistic. He kicked Greg and hit their younger sister whenever they didn't behave as he wanted them to do. He called his mother names and told her husband that he hated his guts. His mother said he was incorrigible and that he was just like his father. Greg supposed she was right—his brother was mean.

Greg's younger sister cried a lot. When she didn't get her own way she hollered and pouted and sobbed until somebody did something to appease her. Greg's stepfather said she was a spoiled brat. Greg's mother agreed and said her daughter was just like her ex-husband. Greg supposed she was right—his sister was selfish.

Greg just kind of blended into the background. He didn't kick or hit. He didn't cry or scream. He simply watched all the scenarios play out before him and learned an awfully lot about how to deal with people. He took on a quiet demeanor and didn't cause any trouble. His mother said he was just like her.

When Greg grew up he married an extroverted, playful woman. He truly thought he loved her. But she was the type to "make waves" in life. She always had a "cause" to march or strike for, and she didn't like anybody telling her what to do. After awhile, she decided she didn't like Greg's quiet ways either—she said he was spineless. She didn't want children. And she wanted to be rich. Greg wanted both, but it wasn't his way to get what he wanted by being loud and boisterous. So he was quiet and waited.

Greg's wife picked at him more and more. She prodded him to get a better job, be more ambitious, and stand up for himself more. Greg's mother said his wife was just like his father. Greg supposed she was right—his wife was sort of mean and selfish.

Greg's wife left him a note on the kitchen table one day. Actually, the note, the table, and Greg's personal belongings were all that was left in the entire house when Greg got home from work that day. His wife informed him that she'd fallen in love with another man—a wealthy entrepreneur—and would file for a divorce from Greg so she could marry the new man in her life quickly.

Greg sat at the table and cried. Tears streamed down his face in rivers of exhausted disappointment and hurt. As he cried, things began moving inside him. His quiet ways turned into a resolve of steel. He *would* take control of life.

Soon after Greg's divorce was final, his father died. Because Greg and his wife had sold their home and split up the money, and since there were no children involved, Greg used his part of the house money to buy out his brother's and sister's share of their father's house. Greg moved back "home" on his thirtieth birthday.

Greg worked steadily over the next years. He seldom dated anyone more than once or did anything socially with others on a continuing basis. But he worked hard. By the time Greg met Ellen on the evening of his thirty-seventh birthday he had amassed thousands of dollars' worth of assets and cash. Nobody was going to control him!

On his first date with Ellen he found that he thoroughly enjoyed her company. Asking her out again couldn't hurt. He enjoyed being with her even more the second time. He liked her quiet ways.

Several months passed and Greg was seeing Ellen frequently. Greg's mother liked Ellen — she said Ellen was just like her. Greg supposed his mother was right — because Ellen seemed a lot like him.

Ellen was an adult child of divorce also. Her mother had left home when Ellen was eight. Ellen's father was heartsick. He never got over losing the only woman he ever loved. He was sullen and full of self-pity much of the time. Basically, he went to work, came home, ate, and watched television in his easy chair until it was time for bed. Ellen basically parented herself and her younger brother.

Their mother remarried and had two more children. Ellen and her brother seldom saw their mother during the rest of their growing-up years. Ellen was a bubbling pot of emotions. She never fully understood why her parents divorced, why her mother left them with their father, or why any of her growing up happened the way it did. But one thing was certain. Ellen learned how to take care of herself.

By the time Ellen was in ninth grade she knew that she would take control of life as soon as she was old enough to be out on her own. She would not live at the mercy of others as an adult.

When Ellen graduated from high school she went from the ceremony at the high school gym to her father's house, loaded her packed suitcases into her old jalopy, and moved into an apartment in a nearby suburb. The only tinge of regret she felt was leaving her younger brother to live alone with their father. But her brother only had two years of high school left and then he'd be on his own too.

Ellen still remembers the day she drove to her new apartment and how exhilarated and free she felt as she let herself in her own front door.

Ellen still went dutifully to her father's or mother's on birthdays and holidays to drop off gifts or to share a meal. Her father still had the same easy chair he'd had when Ellen was a little girl. The only difference was that his children had paid to have it recovered as a gift a few years before.

Ellen seemed to be such a quiet, responsible girl. Yet deep inside her emotions roiled and clashed. She didn't marry, so she didn't have children. She worked as a clerk in a retail store and barely got by financially. The night she met Greg, she was with some of her co-workers, celebrating the retirement of one of them. She saw Greg as he was being seated at his table and thought he was awfully attractive. She stole glances at him off and on throughout the meal.

When she caught him looking at her, she felt a spark of something as their eyes met. Ellen didn't date very often. Lately she'd been thinking more and more that it would be nice to have a male companion, but nothing serious, just sort of a playmate. That evening she made sure to bump into Greg in the foyer as he was preparing to leave.

Now, after dating Greg for many months, Ellen wasn't sure what to think. They didn't make any long-term commitments to each other. But it was an unspoken assumption that neither saw anyone else.

Ellen didn't like Greg's mother. She thought she was a pushy old thing, but she tolerated her because she sensed Greg would have nothing to do with anyone who wouldn't accept his mother.

Greg didn't particularly care for Ellen's father. He seemed to be such an unambitious and spineless man.

Round and Round the Story Goes

Greg and Ellen kept going together as a couple. Both churned deep down inside with untapped emotions bumping and grinding into one another. The only thing that Greg and Ellen were each privately certain about was that *nobody* was going to control *their* lives. They also each believed that if they kept enough control over their emotions and circumstances, happiness would be theirs and nobody could take it away from them. The ironic thing was that they were holding on to control so tightly they were actually out-of-control and *un*happy.

Then Ellen's father died. A few weeks after his funeral, as

Ellen and Greg were putting his household and personal belongings in order, Ellen's emotions finally came gushing to the surface.

She had just sat down for a rest in her father's easy chair. Sitting there, looking at the small world he'd surrounded himself with for twenty-four years, it suddenly seemed that all the hurts, questions, and heartbreak of every one of those years were alive in Ellen's body. Greg watched, horrified, as Ellen dissolved into whimpering sobs of pain.

For more than an hour she cried and demanded answers to questions that were very unnerving to Greg—they hit too close to home. Ellen's loss of control was repulsive to Greg. He couldn't stand the thought of anyone making herself that vulnerable.

Ellen started seeing a counselor and opening up all sorts of wounds that Greg just didn't want to hear about. She tried to tell him about her hurting Piggy-Back Child, and how good it felt to meet her face-to-face. Ellen tried to speak to Greg about really taking control of his own life and happiness rather than trying to make life stand still in his control. Greg wouldn't listen.

Now Greg told Ellen he didn't want to see her anymore. Ellen was devastated on the one hand and relieved on the other. She sensed that she was finally going to make a real life for herself. Greg kept his feelings in tight rein and went on about the business of working even harder than before. His mother said it was just as well that he had dumped Ellen because she was getting too smart for her own good. Greg supposed his mother was right—she always was.

MANAGEMENT: LETTING GO TO FREEDOM

Whether a quest for control is aggressive and demanding or inhibited and manipulative doesn't really matter. The end result is still the opposite of what the goal was in the first place—the questor ends up being *out*-of-control.

In Ellen's case, she chose to let go of her emotions long enough to come full circle and actually gain control of her life but not of life in general. She chose to walk through her pain, release her suffering, and eventually let go to freedom.

Greg, on the other hand, continued to live within a self-imposed emotional prison. He wouldn't let go of his tightly checked control; therefore, he had no real control at all.

Self-discipline is a healthy way to take control of your own life. Self-bondage is an unnecessary punishment. Adult children of divorce are quite often subjected to circumstances that force them to opt for self-bondage in order to survive the crush of their parents' divorces when they were children.

Sadly, however, many ACDs remain in their emotional prisons well into adulthood and long after it is necessary. Their hurting Piggy-Back Children will not let go — they don't know any different way to live other than to aggressively try to take control of their lives or to withdraw from outward reactions and learn to manipulate others in their own quiet ways, all the while trying desperately to maintain control.

To strike a balance of control in your life, it is vital that you be brutally honest with yourself in regard to how you view control and whether or not you are on an unrealistic quest for control.

The balance is struck when you have healthy amounts of self-discipline and freedom governing your life. For instance, if you exercise your freedom to eat whatever you want and you become obese, then your quest for control has led you to be *out*-of-control. On the other hand, if you exercise your freedom to eat whatever you want by using self- discipline to make wise choices for your health and fitness, then you are in control of your life in this area — a balance is struck.

Sometimes we hold on so tightly to habits, behaviors, and beliefs that the only way to gain real freedom from our own tyranny is to *let go* of whatever is, in reality, controlling us.

You may need to let go of many haunting problems from your past that have their beginnings during or after your parents' divorce. How can you let go of dysfunctional relationships, frantic life living, tendencies to extremes, insecurities, great needs for consistency, fears of abandonment, low self- esteem, loneliness, physical ailments, and emotional drains? We'll explore some different ways to do just that.

Letting Go of the Quest

Throughout this book you've had opportunities to look in on people's lives who were affected in one way or another by divorce. Sadly, the impact of parents' divorces on children of all ages can echo long and hard into their adulthood. Regrettably, there is little good to say about how divorce affects children except that there are cases where the home life has been so horrendous children feel relieved when parents separate. But even these kids still feel a deep loss.

The keys to letting go of the negative effects as an adult child of divorce appear to rest in taking the following steps:

1. Purposefully choose to learn to loosen up, relax, and enjoy life.
2. Accept the reality that through the self-discipline to do what's best for you, you can balance having control of your life with your freedom of choice.
3. Accept the truth that there is no magical recipe for guaranteed happiness, health, security, or success in this life.
4. Accept that you can only take control of your life, not of life itself. There are no Edens out there waiting for you to put the right combination together before you can stumble upon it.
5. Try not to deny that your parents' divorce has affected your life.
6. Try not to blame your parents' divorce and the conflicts surrounding it for every small problem you do have.
7. Be honest with yourself about your need for control and try to unearth any manipulative patterns you may use to control others, such as playing on their weaknesses, exaggerating circumstances, or planning emotional traps (withholding love and approval until they do what you want).

8. Beware of allowing finances and material things to become a vehicle for you to control others or keep yourself in tight, emotional rein.

9. Remember that many of the effects you suffer have roots in your parents' divorce. You see the aftermath of it from the perspective of your frightened, confused Piggy-Back Child. All this needs to be integrated with your mature adult self.

10. Accept that becoming a whole, integrated adult may take time, nurturing, and patiently loving yourself.

11. Dare to demand excellence from yourself and face the "messy" emotions you may have to deal with to get completely whole.

12. Finally, realize that you are a child of God and that it is your choice as to whether or not you will accept the freedom, privileges, rewards, and security of this fact. "Letting go" so that God can "grow you up" can be the most tremendous liberation you have ever experienced.

Nancy, thirty-five, discovered the fullness of God's liberation when she least expected it and didn't even realize she'd been looking for it—a year after her divorce.

Nancy's parents divorced when she was twelve. Nancy's father moved just down the street from the family home. All six of the children in the family flowed easily between their father's house and that of their mother. Nancy's parents were careful not to criticize each other in front of the children or to have antagonistic confrontations in their presence. They used a mediator to help them make decisions so that there was a healthy example of the decision-making process and some semblance of the security of a healthy, nuclear family in the kids' lives.

Nancy remembers her mother and father calmly telling the children that, though they once loved each other enough to make a commitment to their marriage forever, certain things had happened. They weren't prepared for these and they no longer loved each other—so they would get a divorce. Both parents emphasized that, although they no longer loved each other, their love for the children remained the same and nothing could ever change that.

Nancy remembers wondering how they could know this for sure, since other things had most definitely happened that they didn't expect and changed the love they once shared. Maybe their feelings for their children would change too. But Nancy also sensed their sincerity and saw by her parents' example following their split that they meant what they said. Nancy doesn't remember hearing a mean word about one from the other. Both Nancy's parents backed each other up in discipline issues, school involvement, and house rules.

It wasn't until Nancy started going through her own divorce, twenty years later, that she went to her mother, Barb, and asked how they'd ever gotten through it so well.

Barb smiled, "I don't know that we did, Nancy. I can't tell you how many times I wanted to just rip your dad to shreds, and I'm sure it worked both ways. There were times I hated him so badly I was sure that his living close to me and haunting my life was God's punishment upon me for getting a divorce."

"You've got to be kidding!" Nancy exclaimed. "The only sense us kids ever got was that you and Dad had the greatest respect for each other and us kids were the most important things in the world!"

"Good," Barb said. "Then it was all worth it and we accomplished what we agreed to do — put you kids first and our own needs second."

"Oh, boy!" Nancy chirped. "I can't believe you felt any hostility toward each other at all! What self-control you must have had!"

"Not control, Nancy, self-discipline. The scariest part of a divorce is losing control. The agony of divorce is so crushing at times that you can temporarily become powerless over everything from finances to whether or not you can sleep at night. The key to success is self-discipline. I think too many couples go into a divorce thinking, *Freedom! Control!* and come out thinking, *Prison! Out-of-control!.* There's just not a whole lot of good about divorce—except relief from the draining pressures of a relationship that doesn't work. Then you find that you have other draining pressures plus the fact that you're alone to deal with them."

"But, Mom," Nancy began, "what else can you do with a relationship that's over? It's not good to live in the middle of tension and depression all the time either!"

"I don't know what to tell you, Nancy, except that if I had it to do over, I probably wouldn't have divorced."

"Because you think God punished you?" Nancy asked bluntly.

"No!" Barb grinned. "No, I realized long ago that God doesn't punish us. He sustains us while we punish ourselves. No, I would stay married to your dad for other reasons—the most important one being to eliminate the damage of tearing a family apart. Even in the most amiable of circumstances, divorce causes emotional destruction in one way or another. Also, think about this—our relationship changed for the worse over a period of time. Couldn't that work the other way? Is it possible we could've fallen in love with each other again for the same or different reasons if we would have waited for a period of time and worked it out?"

"Are you telling me you think I should back out of getting my divorce and try to work it out?" Nancy asked expectantly.

"No, I can't tell you that—only you can make that decision, Nancy. I'm just saying what my experience was. Your father did not abuse me in any way, he was a hard worker, an excellent provider, a good father, and a decent person. We just fell out of love, that's all. When I look back on it, with twenty years in between, mind you, it seems almost silly—we could just as easily have fallen back in love if we had held off on the split for awhile. But once the wheels are set in motion it's very difficult to go back."

Nancy groaned, "If I held off my divorce I'd go totally crazy, Mom! I couldn't stand us being in the same house one more minute!"

"Well, Nancy, you're a big girl now and that's your decision to make."

That evening, after Nancy had tucked her two little guys into bed, she sat down on the couch to read. But her mind kept coming back to what her mother had said, "God sustained me while I punished myself." That had really hit home for Nancy because she'd been feeling so guilty and ashamed about divorcing that she'd been secretly fearing what God might "make her go through" as a consequence.

Nancy kept wondering about the nature of God. She remembered being terrified of Him as a child — all those Sunday school stories from the Old Testament about forcing Adam and Eve out of the garden, making women bear children in terrible pain, sending those awful plagues, and destroying whole cities full of people. Then He seemed to change in the New Testament. After He'd sent His Son to earth it appeared that His love, mercy, and forgiveness were right up front. Nancy wondered if it was God who changed, or His relationship with mankind, or what the difference was.

Nancy couldn't shake all the questions she had about God that were rolling around in her mind. She got a Bible from a shelf and opened it to the New Testament — she liked that better. Nancy flipped through several pages, reading short passages here and there. She knew that marriage and parenting were held in the highest esteem by God. And she supposed she was hoping to find a single verse or phrase that would help her to justify her actions. She couldn't find one.

Nancy struggled with her conscience and thoughts of going through with her divorce. She really did not believe she could put her marriage back together or that she wanted to. After all, God did offer His children free will to make their own choices, didn't He? Of course, but that didn't mean they always made good choices.

Nancy thought about what her mother had said concerning the true feelings between her parents after the divorce, hiding them for the sake of the kids and now wondering if it would have been better not to divorce at all. Uff! Nancy couldn't deal with this tug-of-war within her. And the Bible only seemed to confuse her rather than help her.

As Nancy was about to turn off the lamp and go to bed she reached over to shut the Bible. Her eyes fell on Matthew 7:7 where Jesus said, "Ask and it will be given to you; seek and you will find; knock and the door will be opened to you."

She read it twice. And aloud she said, "Okay, Lord, here I am — asking You for guidance. I am seeking help in this situation and I'm knocking at the door for Your wisdom." Then Nancy went to bed.

By the time she arose the next morning, she had forgotten all about the verse and her prayer. But God didn't forget. He was working diligently behind the scenes. Nancy didn't notice the little things that were influencing the way she was thinking and feeling. She never really connected her conversation with her mother or her evening of looking through the Bible with anything God might be doing in her life.

But over the next several weeks Nancy seemed to "coincidentally" run into all sorts of people who had important things to say about divorce. Nancy supposed it was kind of like test driving a certain kind of car — suddenly the same model seemed to be everywhere you looked. If you were tuned in to something you were bound to be more attentive.

It was an odd thing, though. The people who voiced their various thoughts about divorce all expressed caution and doubt about the wisdom of getting divorced. The reason it seemed odd was that they were mostly people who'd been through divorce. Nancy would have expected them to be more supportive of the positive changes that had happened in their lives. She would've thought they'd talk about their new-found selves, relief from the pressures, and relished independence.

Instead, people were basically telling her she should make sure that the grass which looked greener on the other side of the fence wasn't simply a reflection of the side she was already on.

Nancy decided they just didn't understand — if they were in her shoes they'd go through with a divorce.

As she sat waiting until her attorney could meet with her one afternoon, Nancy was struck by a small plaque that nestled almost out of sight among some books on a shelf. It read, "For lack of guidance a nation falls, but many advisers make victory sure" (Proverbs 11:14).

Before Nancy could think too deeply about this, the receptionist came to get her. The attorney went over a draft of what was to be the final paperwork to submit to the court for consideration in processing the divorce. It seemed a pretty black-and-white situation. Nancy and her soon-to-be-ex-husband had decided on child support, custody, visitation, and division of property in what seemed to be a civilized manner. Nancy glanced over the paperwork, saw that everything was in order, and signed it.

She felt a surge of something she assumed to be power as she backed her car out of a parking space. Soon, Nancy would be in complete control of her life!

Twelve months later, however, Nancy's life was in a shambles around her. She was physically exhausted, emotionally drained, and financially taxed beyond her limits in the aftermath of what had turned out to be a very ugly divorce. Her ex-husband, it turned out, wanted control as much as Nancy did.

As Nancy sat with her mother one morning over tea, she remarked, "I should have listened to you, Mom, and realized that it wasn't going to be easy. I should've known I wouldn't be the exception to the rule. I can't believe how many people tried to advise me!"

Barb smiled sadly. "I think the hardest part about really growing up is the acceptance that none of us is the exception to the rule. And yet we are each special and unique in our own way. I'm sorry you're having such a tough time, Nancy. I wouldn't wish it on anybody!"

"Me either!" Nancy declared. "From now on, I'll be the first one to discourage others from rushing into divorce! You wake up one day—and Bam!—you've ruined your life!"

"Oh, no, Nancy!" Barb quickly replied. "You haven't ruined your life. You have a chance to start new and fresh each day! Remember, God doesn't punish you for wrong choices. He sustains you until you let go of the guilt and bad stuff so He can help you get on with the business of making a new life for yourself and your children. It won't be easy—the natural consequences of our wrong moves never are—but you'll come out a much stronger person for it!"

"I don't know, Mom," Nancy said. "I feel like a rag that somebody's rung out nearly dry. Instead of being in control, I'm just the opposite."

"Okay, Nancy, let me give you something to hang on to while God is working with you." Barb went to her desk across the room and got out a piece of paper laminated in plastic. She handed it to Nancy, "Read this every time you want to give up!"

Nancy read:

To Whom it May Concern:
"Though your sins are like scarlet, they shall be as white as snow; though they are red as crimson, they shall be like wool"
(Isaiah 1:18).
Because:
"All have sinned and fall short of the glory of God"
(Romans 3:23).
But:
"Those who hope in the Lord will renew their strength. They will soar on wings like eagles; they will run and not grow weary, they will walk and not be faint" (Isaiah 40:31).

When Nancy looked up, her eyes glistened with tears. "Well, I didn't listen last time to wise counsel, and I'm sure I'll make wrong choices again, but I have a feeling that I'll never be quite as naive or so quick to run from God's attempts to get my attention!"

"Let's put it this way," Barb said gently, "the only sure way to be in control is to be in His care. We have to trust enough to let go to Him. You'll never be the same again, Nancy. All this struggle and heartbreak will change you, but it can make you a better, wiser, and more fulfilled person!"

It can seem a nearly insurmountable task to put the pieces of our lives together — over and over again. We may have to try to climb thousands of sandpiles in our lives — some much bigger than others.

But for the adult children of divorce, a choice to attempt the climb is the only real one to make. Because to make no choice in regard to growth and health is actually a choice *not* to grow or become healthier!

You can move through pain and immobilization to fulfillment and freedom — regardless of how heavy a burden your Piggy-Back Child may seem right now — to find your place in life!

Try the next exercise to help you determine what that particular place may be at present.

Exercise: Finding Your Place in Life

Taking on a quest to control life is an impossible task. There is no way you can control all of life circumstances that will affect you. But you can be in control of your own life.

In fact, the deeper struggle when control is quested after is actually a desperate attempt to find your place in life. Maybe you were secure in your place as a child — until your parents divorced. And then you were ejected from your place and never found a safe, comfortable one again. Instead of searching for your place in a healthy manner, you may have decided to try to force the world to offer you a place by trying to control life itself!

There are three imperative steps to take as you begin to find your place in life:

1. Realize that you do have one! Romans 8:28 says, "And we know that in all things God works for the good of those who love him, who have been called according to his purpose."
2. Believe that you are worthy of your place in life!
3. Seek out what your place is.

An exercise to help you begin your search follows. The sample is already filled out for a man we'll call Dwayne. Using his example as a guide, get paper and pencil for yourself and sit at a comfortable table or desk. Then fill in your own personal list:

What I Do or Should Be Doing:

1. Go to my job every day.
2. Keep up the house and yard.
3. Run errands and supervise kids.
4. Should do exercises.
5. Should do more with my kids.
6. Should relax more.
7. Should be more active with the needy.
8. Should visit relatives more.
9. Should save more money.
10. Should be more grateful for what I have.
11. Should be more religious .
12. Should be more understanding of my wife.

What I Like or Would Like to Do:

1. I'd like a different job .
2. I'd like to spend more time on my home and garden.
3. I'd like to eliminate some of my time spent on errands.
4. I'd like to relax more.
5. I'd like to take better care of myself physically.
6. I'd like to get the pressure to perform off me.
7. I'd like to make a living at something more fulfilling.
8. I'd like to spend more pleasurable time with my kids.
9. I'd like to spend more enjoyable time with my spouse.
10. I'd like to have more savings.

Now, make the same two kinds of lists for yourself.

Dwayne is obviously family oriented. Your lists may have more to do with your individual do's, shoulds, likes, and needs. Either way — *Your place in life is where you like to be!*

Not everything you do in life will truly be enjoyable — we all have unpleasant or distasteful tasks to do. But the bulk of your life can fall in the "like" category.

It's important that you take the time, right now, to begin transforming your life into one that's "likeable" and fits you! Tomorrow may be too late — remember, you can't control life, but you can be in control of your own.

For instance, in Dwayne's exercise, he took (and you can take) the following steps:

1. Eliminate every single "should" on your list. Where is it a law that you "should" see your relatives more often, save more money, or be more religious? What do these things mean anyway? How often is often enough? How much is enough?

Guilt over what we think we "should" do in life seems to be one of the most destructive and pervasive forces there is. Get rid of it! You are who you are, and finding your place in life means finding out where you are uniquely comfortable — and that's between you and God!

2. Realize and believe that when you're in your place, the others in your life will become better adjusted and healthy also. For example, your wife may hate to hear you say you're going to implement a plan to switch careers because she is fearful of change or negative repercussions. But if your plan is practical and you follow it in logical steps to fruition, your wife will most likely be delighted to see the new you who enjoys being in your own niche! When you're happy, those around you are more apt to be happy!

3. *Don't forget a plan!* Nobody is advocating that a $30-per-hour union worker comes home one day and says, "Honey, I've decided to quit my job and start a band! We'll have to live on love and faith for a few years." Rather, sit down first by yourself, then with your spouse, then with your children, and finally with any professionals you may need help from (accountant, attorney, banker, or counselor) and go through a realistic plan of how

you can change a 9-to-5 job you really aren't happy with into a career you love. If you're doing something you love, your energy and enthusiasm often carries you naturally into a place where you have adequate income.

4. Accept that there are sacrifices to be made in order to find your "likeable" place in life. You may have to sacrifice money, time, the approval of others, and maybe some of your old routines that you hesitate to give up because they're comfortable and difficult to change.

5. In Dwayne's exercise, after the "shoulds" are crossed off, only three things remain: work, home, and family duties. In the "like" column are those things that involve both the three items already being done and the things that are important enough to want to do them. Take the things from the "like" column and address the issues in writing, one at a time.

For example, Dwayne's job is brought up directly and indirectly in both his lists — apparently his job isn't very fulfilling and demands so much time and energy that it prevents him from doing the other things he wants to do in life. So, "Job" is the main issue. Following that would be the issue of "More Time" with home, garden relaxation, physical health, kids, and wife. Next would be the issue of "Less Time" on errands and routine things. Finally, the issue of "Saving More Money."

Write each of your own issues at the top of separate pages.

6. Now you can begin to brainstorm options you have, ideas you come up with, and possibilities to consider in regard to making your life a "Likeable Place." As a sample, we'll brainstorm Dwayne's "Job" issue:

Job (Assembler in a Factory)

What I like about my job:
　　The people

What I dislike about my job:
　　Too many hours
　　Too structured

Too fast-paced
Not creatively challenging

What jobs/businesses I think I would like more:
Wood carver
Furniture maker
Crafts gallery owner

Why I think I would like these:
Slower pace
Less structure
Creative
My own endeavor

What keeps me from trying these:
Not available in my area
Less money in job position
Money risk in own business

Where could I get information and help to research the possibilities of trying something new and eliminating the things that hold me back?
Vocational counseling
A Chamber of Commerce
Banker
Employment service
College
Yellow Pages
Business and Professional Directories
Ads for local hobby clubs and items I'm
interested in

When will I begin to seek this help?:
Next week

You can brainstorm each issue in this manner by addressing:
1. What you like about how you are now.

2. What you dislike about your present situation.
3. What you think you'd like more.
4. Why you think so.
5. What keeps you from changing.
6. Ways you could change and where you could get help.
7. When you will begin to make changes.
8. Remember, nothing is written in blood—you don't have to make a major life change, you're just trying out some ideas! Don't let fears of being out of control stop you from brainstorming—you can stay exactly as you are if you choose. That's what being in control of your life means—having the freedom and power to choose. Just because you may discuss with your banker or the local Chamber of Commerce the possibility of opening a business doesn't mean you have to do it!
9. Try different plans, ideas, and brainstorms as often as you become aware of an area of your life where you're feeling you "should" be doing something. Sort through the issues of your life periodically, finding the places you fit at various times in your life.

As we end this part of your journey as an adult child of divorce, or as one who is close to those affected by divorce, I would like to add one final message from a personal perspective.

A Final Note

To do the best job possible, writers must put themselves mentally and emotionally within the people they're describing temporarily. This can be a very challenging thing at times. I am compelled to tell you that this has been the most emotionally stirring—and painful—book I've written.

Divorce is a serious choice we make for ourselves. All legal and spiritual issues aside, it is a tearing apart of something very precious—our families.

As the keepers of our children's well-being, we have a grave responsibility. It is my opinion, after completing this project, that we should go to extremely great lengths to preserve our marriages. Trial separations, counseling and extensive soul-searching should all take place.

If these attempts fail, and divorce is the final decision, then I believe it is imperative that professional counseling and mediation services be used to aid the members of the torn family network to put the pieces of their lives back together again.

The love and support of extended family members and friends is deeply needed during and after a divorce. Grandparents, aunts, uncles, cousins, neighbors, teachers, and friends can all give invaluable stability and encouragement for the healthy adjustment of the children who must experience the traumas of divorce.

We all need each other. And we need to learn to make choices in favor of our well-being. We need to reach out beyond our narrow, individual worlds to connect with one another. In this way, we buoy up ourselves and become better people. We choose excellence.

You may have noticed that several of the ACDs, their spouses, or children in the book exhibited tendencies toward perfectionism. We must not confuse excellence with perfection! Perfection simply does not exist in this world — it is an idyllic fabrication of our minds. It is important that individuals, who feel driven by perfectionism, accept that the best thing they can do for themselves is to strive for excellence in their lives.

Many couples choose divorce believing it will be the answer to their problems. They mistakenly believe that by divorcing they will be better, more secure and loving people. It has been my discovery that this is not necessarily true. And it is rarely the case for the children. Life after divorce can become extraordinarily more difficult and painful than it was before. Divorce needs to be thought through and discussed with others who can be objectively helpful over a long period of time before it is actually chosen as an end.

I hope that as an adult child of divorce, you will make good choices for yourself. I hope that you will choose to learn more about why you are who you are. And I trust that you will be able to integrate the negative effects of growing up with divorce into your adult personality in ways that foster your wholeness—and your inner joy. When life looks bleak, and you feel that you cannot cope with the burden of making yourself whole, remember Jesus' words in Mark 10:27, "With man this is impossible, but not with God; all things are possible with God."

Endnotes

Introduction

1. Judith S. Wallerstein and Sandra Blakeslee, *Second Chances: Men, Women and Children a Decade after Divorce* (New York: Ticknor & Fields, 1989) p. 303.
2. Harold J. Sala, *Today Can Be Different* (Ventura, CA: Regal Books, 1988) November 11.

Chapter 1

1. Lloyd John Ogilvie, *God's Transforming Love* (Ventura, CA: Regal Books, 1988) p. 7.
2. Julie Bawden Davis, "Marital Strife," *Orange Coast Magazine* 172 (1990): 172–175.

Chapter 8

1. "After Words," with Jane Wallace; Lifetime Television: "Your Family Matters" (3-7-90). Written and produced by Michael Tanaka.
2. Ibid.
3. "Don't Divorce the Children," with Tim Busfield; Lifetime Television: "Your Family Matters" (3-7-90). Inspired by "Helping Your Child Succeed After Divorce" by Frances Bienenfeld (Hunter House). Produced by Dina DeLuca.

Chapter 9

1. "Ten Tips for Teens," Message by Dr. Robert Schuller (Garden Grove, CA: 1989). Used by permission of Robert Schuller Ministries.